Vermont Walks: Village and Countryside

Walking Tours of Forty-Three Vermont Villages And Their Surroundings

❦

Written by
MARILYN STOUT
Illustrated by
JANET FREDERICKS

SPECIAL THANKS

This book of village and countryside walks
was made possible by very generous financial
contributions from:

The A.D. Henderson Foundation
Claneil Foundation
Blue Cross-Blue Shield of Vermont
The Windham Foundation
The National Trust for Historic Preservation

This book is published by: Vermont Life Magazine,
6 Baldwin Street, Montpelier, VT 05602;
in association with: Preservation Trust of Vermont,
104 Church Street, Burlington, VT 05401.

Designed by Carol Hanley,
Hanley Design, Charlotte, VT

Printed in the U.S.A. by Queen City Printers, Burlington, VT

First edition, August, 1995.

Library of Congress Cataloging-in-Publication Data
Stout, Marilyn.
Vermont walks: village and countryside: walking tours of forty-
    three Vermont villages and their surroundings / written by
    Marilyn Stout; illustrated by Janet Fredericks. — 1st ed.
    p. cm.
    ISBN 0-936896-41-8
    1. Vermont — Tours. 2. Walking — Vermont — Guidebooks.
        3. Villages — Vermont — Guidebooks. I. Title.
    F47.3.S76 1995   917.4304'43 — dc20   95-33286   CIP

Introduction

VERMONT IS PERENNIALLY referred to as "unique," a place apart, a "special" place, and most Vermonters instinctively feel that it is.

But what does that really mean? What is actually unique about Vermont, if anything?

Vermont's mountains are not the highest or most spectacular in North America. Likewise, there are many other places that are farmed—and many other farming states have larger and more prosperous farms than Vermont. Vermont doesn't have the largest or most powerful cities in America by a long shot.

And yet most Vermonters and many of the thousands of people who visit here annually feel immediately the indefinable something that sets this small, green state apart. What is it?

The 18th century English poet William Whitehead was faced with a similar problem in writing a poem extolling the indefinable charm of Celia, a young woman he had fallen in love with. In a poem entitled, "The Je Ne Sais Quoi," or "The I-know-not-what," Whitehead declared that it wasn't her face, her figure, her voice or any other single aspect of Celia that bewitched him. "Her voice, her touch, might give the alarm ," he wrote,

> *. . .'Twas both, perhaps, or neither.*
> *In short, 'twas that provoking charm*
> *Of Celia altogether.*

Those of us who love Vermont have come, more than once, to just that conclusion. It's not any one thing: it's everything.

It's the fabric of small-town life and the closeness of farms and unspoiled nature; the echo of the crystal stream through the forest, and the knowledge that soon your walk will bring you to your own front door. It's the familiarity of traditional buildings: the white church on the village green, covered bridges, barns in working fields close by small, livable towns. All of these elements create the palpable sense of a vibrant past combined with an equally vibrant present.

Visually, Vermont's charm is expressed in the interplay of village and countryside that makes our landscape pastoral. That interplay, the rolling, beautiful landscape that includes farmland, villages and forested mountainsides is, in fact, what Vermont has that is unique.

We don't have a Grand Canyon, as Arizona does. We don't have the Rocky Mountains of Colorado, or the Mississippi River, or San Francisco or the beaches of Cape Cod. But we do have a landscape that speaks of two hundred years of human cooperation with nature, the land and the weather.

We have the view of Mount Mansfield from Pleasant Valley. Looking south from Cambridge or Underhill, the peak of Mount Mansfield looms dramatically above the nearby farms, and makes the entire view deeper and stronger. The presence of those farms enhances and strengthens our view of the mountain because they give us a sense of humanity's place in the picture. We humans belong to nature, that view says: we have a right to be here, and a duty to work with and protect the natural world that shelters and provides for us.

The same could be said of dozens of other familiar vistas: the view of Lake Champlain from the farmed highlands of Charlotte along Route 7, the view of Newbury and the Connecticut River Valley from Mount Pulaski, the dramatic view of Mount Equinox as it rises almost directly above Manchester. And so on.

We are fortunate that such views are commonplace. And yet Vermont is much more than a state with beautiful vistas. It is also a state of villages. Villages and small cities.

We Vermonters do not realize how lucky we are to still have workable towns and cities. In much of the rest of the country, small, delightful places like Peacham and Montpelier and Pawlet have been wrecked by strip development and runaway highways. We have all seen such relics, sadly overrun by fast-food restaurants and car dealerships on frantically busy highways to somewhere else. And we are all glad to return to the cohesiveness of Vermont, a place where villages still work.

In North Bennington, for example, there's a true national treasure, the Park-McCullough House, a Victorian masterpiece. Yet there are humbler glories as well. The old mills, the worker housing (now converted to middle-class homes) the village store and other commercial buildings all have their stories to tell of days gone by—and also function as part of contemporary North Bennington. The village is a delightful collection of all kinds of architecture and is unique. Also unique is the fact that just a short walk down a couple of village streets brings the walker immediately into open fields and classic pastoral countryside.

Or consider Brownington, one of the little-known gems of the Northeast Kingdom. Walk from the Old Stone House—a massive grey stone building that was an early grammar school dormitory and is now a museum—down the town's central street toward the white-steepled hillside church at its northerly end. The home of the Rev. Alexander Twilight, the man who built the Old Stone House and ran the Brownington School, is nearby, and the entire village looks much as it did when Twilight kept school here. In the cemetery beside the little church, you will find his grave, and that of his wife, Mercy.

Follow the path up the hill beside the church to an observatory tower at the top. From the tower, there's yet another striking view. Beyond the little village of Brownington, an array of mountains and lakes, farms and forested hillsides spreads out in all directions. To the south, the peaks of Pisgah and Mount Hor rise above Lake Willoughby. It's a lovely view and it could exist nowhere but here.

Vermont is like that: one minute, a village street; the next, all outdoors. It's the mixture that is the hallmark of our state. The fabric woven of those experiences is what has lodged it in the affections of its people and the nation.

However, that raises a problem. It's easy to understand the value of a Grand Canyon or a mountain range, or even a wildflower. They're immediate and definable. But it's hard to define, let alone promote or appreciate a "fabric"—something as subtle as a mixture of village, wilderness, and pastoral landscape. Nevertheless, if the Je Nais Sais Quoi of Vermont is to be saved, people need to learn to appreciate it, know that it's fragile, and protect it.

Which is where this book comes in.

The walks included in this volume, in addition to being healthful and pleasant, are designed to show you how Vermont's incomparable landscape "works." They are not mountain hikes through Green Mountain wilderness, but modest walks aimed at helping the walker appreciate the everyday beauty that is Vermont. Most of them include both a tour of the village at hand and a walk through the surrounding countryside.

That is by design. It is our contention that Vermont landscape is a partnership involving both humanity and nature; that it is a near ideal mixture of them, and that each benefits from the presence of the other.

We invite you to sample the walks presented in this book. If they help you to get to know Vermont better, and to care about her landscape, villages, and historic resources more deeply, the book will have served its purpose.

TOM SLAYTON, EDITOR
VERMONT LIFE MAGAZINE

PAUL BRUHN, EXECUTIVE DIRECTOR
PRESERVATION TRUST OF VERMONT

A Note to Walkers

Vermont is the safest state in the nation, but not if you walk down the middle of the highway. Most of the walks in this book include sections of public roads, some of which will have traffic. On busy roads, please walk on the left, facing traffic, and stay well out of the way of oncoming cars. Wear light/ bright colors and don't walk at dusk or when visibility is severely obscured. In short, use common sense.

The walks are designed to be enjoyed. Do as much or as little of any particular walk as you care to. Some of the longer options are several miles in length, and it is always better to turn back and arrive home re-freshed, rather than walking to the point of blisters and exhaustion. Some of the simpler village walks, indicated in the text by the word, "explore the village," or a similar phrase, are delightful by themselves. Start the season with shorter walks, building up to longer excursions.

Wear comfortable shoes and clothing. Hiking boots are not normally necessary, but a rain jacket might be a good idea on cloudy days, and a bottle of water in sunny weather. Don't overburden yourself with either cares or equipment. The joy of walking is its simplicity.

• Highgate

• Isle La Motte

• Brownington

• Fairfield

• Craftsbury Common

• Johnson
• Greensboro

• Hyde Park

• Burlington • Stowe

• Guildhall

• Shelburne
• Montpelier

• St. Johnsbury

• Waitsfield

• Peacham

• Brookfield
• Newbury

• Chelsea

• Middlebury

• Shoreham
• Strafford

• Orwell
• East Barnard

• Woodstock

• Proctor

• Plymouth Notch

Middletown Springs •
• Wallingford

Pawlet •

Rupert •
Weston •

• Dorset • Landgrove

Manchester Village •
Windham • • Chester

Grafton •

• Bellows Falls

• Townshend

• North Bennington

• Bennington
• Brattleboro

Contents

Northern Vermont

Brownington......8
Burlington......10
Craftsbury Common......12
Fairfield......14
Greensboro......16
Guildhall......18
Highgate......20
Hyde Park......22
Isle La Motte......24
Johnson......26
St. Johnsbury......28
Shelburne......30
Stowe......32

Central Vermont

Brookfield......34
Chelsea......36
East Barnard......38
Middlebury......40
Montpelier......42
Newbury......44
Orwell......46
Peacham......48
Proctor......50
Shoreham......52
Strafford......54
Waitsfield......56
Woodstock......58

Southern Vermont

Bellows Falls......60
Bennington......62
Brattleboro......64
Chester......66
Dorset......68
Grafton......70
Landgrove......72
Manchester Village......74
Middletown Springs......76
North Bennington......78
Pawlet......80
Plymouth Notch......82
Rupert & West Rupert......84
Townshend......86
Wallingford......88
Weston......90
Windham & South Windham......92

Brownington

*T*HE NORTHEAST KINGDOM, the three northeast counties of Vermont, can seem a long way from the 20th century, and nowhere more so than in the calm of Brownington. Only a few miles off a main route, it is sited on a high upland and seems far away in place and time. Paved roads end, and two dirt roads lined with maples meet in a T at the old village center, a 19th-century farming community with fields and mountains falling away on all sides.

An early settlement in Orleans County, Brownington was chartered in 1780. The village grew along the Timothy Hinman Road, a stage route cut in 1791 through the wilderness between Greensboro, Vermont, and Stanstead, Quebec. In 1823 residents chose to establish the county grammar school here, something which left an indelible mark on this community thanks to efforts of the Rev. Alexander Twilight, the school's determined headmaster.

Reverend Twilight is credited with somehow financing and building the commanding, four-story granite dormitory and school for which Brownington is best known today. Working against the wishes of his board of trustees, the legendary Twilight, thought to be the first African American to graduate from an American college (Middlebury College), is said to have quarried stone from the fields and erected this structure largely by himself. It was the first building constructed of Vermont granite.

The imposing gray dormitory, now called the Old Stone House, recalls the mills built in southern New England about the same time, but this structure overlooks sweeping fields. Now the Orleans County Historical Museum, the 25 rooms are full of objects and furnishings from the county, and out back, open for use, is a restored two-hole privy with half-moon doors. (The museum is open daily 11-5 July and August; Fri.-Tue. May 15-June 30 and Sept. 1-Oct. 15; fee charged.)

Reverend Twilight's gravestone is down the road in the hillside cemetery next to the white frame Congregational church (1841).

Walkers who follow a narrow road uphill beside the church have a unique survey of the countryside from a two-story lookout on the hill behind the village. This re-creation of the original Prospect Hill Observatory, which Twilight built for his students, affords expansive views of the Northeast Kingdom's rocky, rolling landscape of open fields and wooded hills, with the Green Mountains and Jay Peak rising in the west, Lake Memphremagog to the north, Willoughby Gap to the southeast, and, on a clear day, the White Mountains in the east. The wooded hillsides circling the village are evidence that the thin soil of former hill farms is depleted, their days now gone. Brownington remains as an echo of that past.

In 1823 residents chose to establish the county grammar school here.
A commanding four-story structure, it was the first building constructed of Vermont granite
and has left an indelible mark on this community.

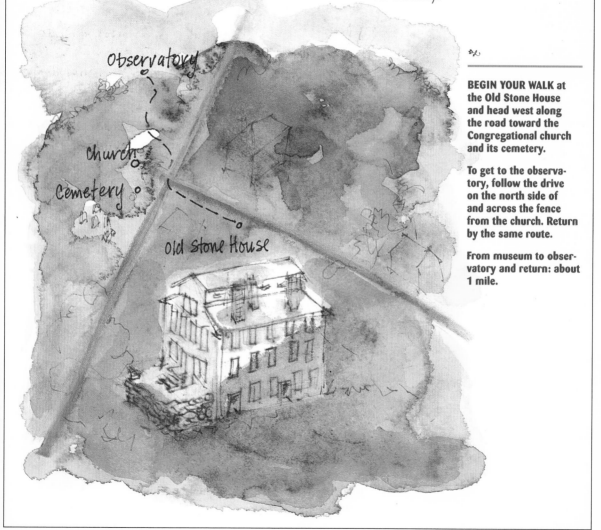

BEGIN YOUR WALK at the Old Stone House and head west along the road toward the Congregational church and its cemetery.

To get to the observatory, follow the drive on the north side of and across the fence from the church. Return by the same route.

From museum to observatory and return: about 1 mile.

Burlington

*T*HE MOST DRAMATIC WAY to arrive in Burlington is by water. The ferry crosses Lake Champlain, 12 miles wide at this point, and the city stretches along the waterfront of the bay and up a hill to the University of Vermont. Although now the largest city in Vermont, with about 38,000 people, Burlington started as a small lakeside village.

The first settlements were at Burlington Bay and over the hill, via what is now Pearl Street and Colchester Avenue, at the Winooski River falls. In the first U.S. census of 1791, the fledgling town had 332 residents.

Burlington began its growth as a port in the 1820s and 1830s after canals opened connecting Lake Champlain with Canada, the Hudson River and the Erie Canal. In the early 20th century, textile mills were added to its industrial mix. Many mills closed after World War II, and with the growth of a large regional hospital and colleges, the city became a service and education center. It also has enjoyed the economic boon provided by a major IBM facility, established in nearby Essex Junction in 1957.

The small Burlington of the early 1800s is traceable today near where it started, the waterfront. The brick house of founder Gideon King (1798) is still at 35 King Street, restored for offices. It is thought to be the oldest building in Burlington. Two blocks of Battery Street (between Maple and Main Streets) are lined with early 19th-century waterfront buildings.

The Old Stone Store at 171 Battery, erected in 1827 as headquarters for the mercantile and shipping firm of Timothy Follett, has massive walls of Isle La Motte limestone floated down the lake by barge. Follett's 1840 mansion, with its monumental columns, presides over the old waterfront on a hill set back from Battery at College Street. At 202 Battery is the original Merchants' Bank building (1850), built with a part-granite facade to imply the bank's stability and the security of its growing commercial accounts.

There is much more to explore throughout the rest of Burlington. Several blocks east of the waterfront is the historic commercial district around City Hall Park and Church Street, now a pedestrian mall. On up the hill 19th-century brick mansions line South Willard, South Union, and Summit streets. Notable houses from the early to late 19th century can be seen along Pearl Street as it passes the Unitarian church (1815) on up to the university green. A row of early workers' housing from the 1830s is on George Street off lower Pearl.

At the foot of College Street, the new Community Boathouse and waterfront park are a new focal point for the community. Here you can step onto the Burlington equivalent of a country lane: a paved, 9-mile bike path that winds along the lake in a sweeping arc through neighborhoods, parks, and woods, often with wide-angle views across the lake to the Adirondack Mountains.

At the foot of College Street, the new Community Boathouse and waterfront park are a new focal point for the community.

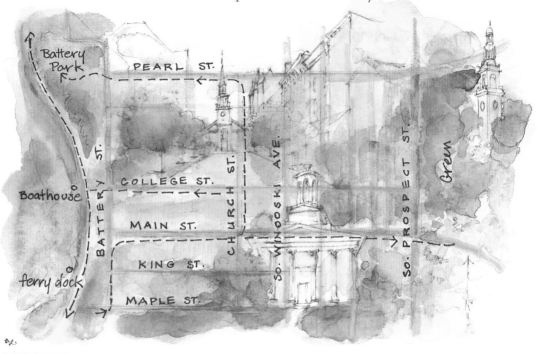

BEGIN YOUR WALK at Battery and Maple streets near the ferry dock. From here you can explore the old waterfront neighborhood or head north to Main Street and turn right to begin a walk up the hill a quarter mile to the historic commercial district at Church Street.

From here it is easy to explore more of the city since the streets form a grid plan, and walking downhill will return you to the waterfront.

Uphill from Church Street are the Hill Section neighborhood and beyond that the University of Vermont, with its impressive green (a half mile up the hill).

If instead you head up to the Unitarian church at the end of Church Street and turn left on Pearl Street, you will return to Battery Street at Battery Park, where there is an inspiring view of the lake.

On Battery Street one block north of Main, you can turn down College Street to the Community Boathouse and the Burlington Bike Path. The path is 9 miles one way, end to end (from the boathouse about 2 miles one way south and 7 miles one way north).

Craftsbury Common

CLIMB TO THE PLATEAU where the white village of Craftsbury Common surrounds a great, sweeping common, the largest in Vermont.

This village has always been distinctive. It was the first settlement in northeast Vermont, a wilderness in 1787 when a group from Massachusetts laid out lots in an orderly plan that still defines the boundaries of many properties. In early years it shared shire town status with Brownington, and its commerce thrived. But after the Civil War most commercial activity migrated down the hill to be near the mills of Craftsbury village, established around the waterpower of the Black River.

At one end of the common, the United Church of Craftsbury retains its original 1820 form and proportion though remodeled several times. Lining another corner, the cluster of Craftsbury Academy structures includes buildings moved to the site as needed, such as the 1858 East Craftsbury Church (used as a gym) and an 1870 one-room schoolhouse. South of the common, a roomy inn from 1840 is now the administration building for two-year Sterling College, and one of the original residences of 1810, later a summer home, is now an inn.

A walk from Craftsbury Common to East Craftsbury crosses high ridge country farmed since the early days. Today, although many farmhouses are second homes, fields still surround the villages, and the town remains largely an agricultural community. The heights on this route still offer stunning views across the fields.

East Craftsbury grew along the Bayley-Hazen Military Road, blazed in 1777. For many years its few buildings nestled among the extensive landholdings of the Simpson family, preserving its pastoral tone.

The flavor of East Craftsbury is captured by the John Woodruff Simpson Memorial Library (Wed. and Sat. 9-12, 2-5, 7-9:30; Sun. 12:15-1:30), once the Simpson's general store. In 1921 Miss Jean Simpson, as she was always called with affection, converted the store into a library and named it for her father, who had left this tiny place to make his fortune in New York City. Miss Jean, an accomplished New Deal administrator, eventually returned here to lead a long and active, community-spirited life. The hitching posts at the store/library remain, and inside the carpeted and wallpapered interior the store shelves are full of books. The counter serves as the librarian's desk.

In the 1980s, after Miss Jean's death, Brassknocker Farm's 800 acres were saved from unplanned development by arrangement with the Vermont Land Trust. The trust sold several clustered building lots and was able to keep most of the land open and undeveloped, thereby maintaining the character of this rural village.

This village, surrounded by a great, sweeping common, has always been distinctive. It was the first settlement in northeast Vermont.

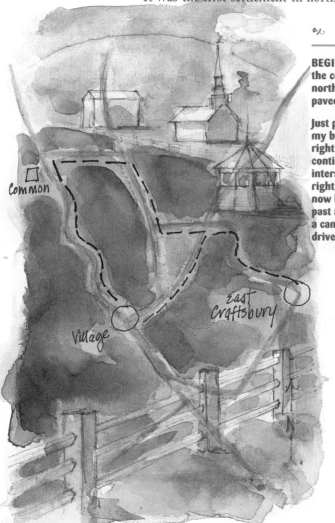

BEGIN YOUR WALK at the common, and head north along the main paved road.

Just past the new academy building, make a right onto a dirt road, continue downhill to a T intersection, and make a right again. (You will now be heading south past a unique barn with a canted-angle, "high-drive" bridge.)

Go downhill about three-quarters of a mile to the next intersection and make a left heading east. Continue across a bridge, through the next intersection, and curve in an S up a steep hill.

Stay on this road, straight, for over another half mile to East Craftsbury village. Return by the same route. (From Craftsbury Common to East Craftsbury and return: 5.4 miles.)

(For an alternate route back, turn left [south] at the bottom of the steep hill, before crossing the bridge, and proceed into Craftsbury village. Then take a right and wind up the hill back to the common. This will add about an extra 1.5 miles to the walk.)

Fairfield

THAT COWS GRAZE on one corner in the center of Fairfield is not surprising—this is a farming community. Sharing the center of the village are a few historic commercial buildings and a modern brick school, which uses the town green as a soccer and baseball field. Surrounding the village are tilled fields and rolling pastureland.

The town of Fairfield was settled around 1787 by people from Fairfield, Connecticut. In the early 19th century the village had a mill, a tannery, churches, town hall, shops, and a tavern. By the middle of the century the town had more than 2,000 residents, and many of the buildings in the center of the village were built about that time. President Chester A. Arthur was born in 1830 a few miles north of the village, where his father was pastor of a church. The site is marked by a re-creation of his birthplace, the original structure having long since disappeared.

With a little imagination, a visitor to the village of Fairfield today can see what it was like a hundred years ago: Many of the buildings are still here. On the center corner is a handsome little store, built around 1830 and in business until 1940. Its orange-red bricks are laid in Flemish bond, a design of alternate short ends and long sides, and it has a semi-circular window above a second-story loading door and a hoisting hood in the peak of the roof. The 1850 clap-boarded building next door also has vestiges of its commercial past, including a pulley in the gable over its loading door. On the southwest corner, next to the green, stands the 1809 Town House, remodeled in 1896 and since used as a school.

Down the south road stands a white clapboard church built in 1864, its pointed-arch windows and door marking its style as Gothic Revival. Further down, there is a low, white-painted brick house (1830) with a graceful rounded window over its paneled door. This was the parsonage for the Congregational church that stood on the green until 1935.

Local stores have declined as residents have become more mobile and a highway paved to nearby St. Albans. Fairfield village is much less commercial than it was even 50 years ago. Still, it lies in the heart of Vermont's top agricultural county, Franklin County. The cropland, pasture, and woodlots of active farms define the surrounding landscape, and the line of peaks in the east lets you know this is the Green Mountain State.

With a little imagination, a visitor to the village of Fairfield today can see what it was like a hundred years ago: Many of the buildings are still here.

BEGIN YOUR WALK at the center of the village. Explore to the south and east as you please, and then stroll north less than a block to the small brick town clerk's office and turn left onto Church Road.

Proceed out Church Road past the early-20th-century Catholic church and cemetery as far as you like and return.

Greensboro

GREENSBORO IS A SUMMER TOWN. In July and August a quiet invasion crests the hill road from the south and disappears into the woods around Caspian Lake, where families open up lakeside camps often owned for generations. Although much of this invasion is hidden from the casual visitor, it can be glimpsed by observing the swirl of activity in Willey's Store and scanning the wall of notices for chamber music concerts and church suppers outside its door. And a look out over the serene blue lake sheltered by hills will explain why this village has drawn summer people for a century.

Chartered in 1781, Greensboro was settled along the Bayley-Hazen Military Road, which was hewn through the wilderness in 1776, but never completed and never used for an intended invasion of Canada. There is a marker at the site of a blockhouse on the west side of the lake where two soldiers were killed by Indians the same year the town was chartered. By 1790 the village at the outlet of Caspian Lake had a sawmill, gristmill, and blacksmith shop. Fires in the early 1800s destroyed most of its buildings, but a later wave of Scottish immigrants built a hotel, stores, new mills, and a school. Summer people began coming in the 1890s, and the flurry of camp building continued into the 20th century.

In the village several town roads meet at a little green that marks the site of the bygone hotel. Nearby are the large square town hall (formerly the high school); the Church of Christ, with its open arched belfry; many green-shuttered white houses; and the rambling Willey's general store, a prime example of its breed. All were built or enlarged in the late 19th or early 20th century.

Until 1896 only a few farmhouses and fishing shacks populated the lakeshore. Then two friends from Burlington who had vacationed in the area, one a minister, bought land for family cottages. A Boston textbook publisher also purchased land, selling it off in camp lots to his clients. The resulting summer colony continued to attract educators and ministers. Some camps were refinements of the existing fishing shacks. All intruded as little as possible on nature, with even two-story boathouses built in a rustic style.

Located at an elevation of 1,463 feet in the Northern Highlands geographic region, Greensboro has distinct seasons, including vivid fall color and a severe winter. Caspian Lake freezes over in winter and remains cool throughout the summer. Despite the short growing season and hilly terrain, small-scale or part-time farming continues, including some sheep farming and dairying. Summer people and those who have retired here now own some of the old farmhouses, so the fragile equilibrium between the land and the people is maintained with new caretakers. There may be fewer meadows and more woods, but pastoral vistas endure.

Summer people began coming in the 1890s, and the flurry of camp building continued into the 20th century. There may be fewer meadows and more woods, but pastoral vistas endure.

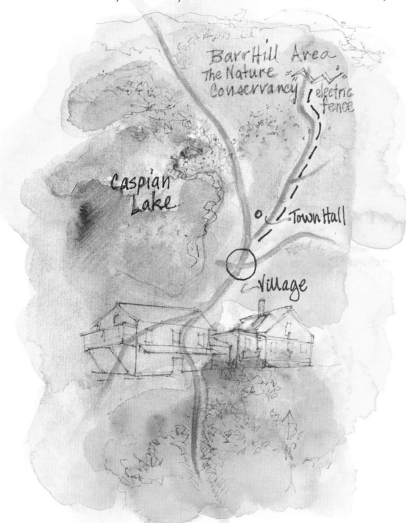

BEGIN YOUR WALK at Willey's Store and explore the center of the village. A short street heads north to the lake and a public beach. Following a good map, you can take a 7-mile walk around the lake on paved and dirt roads.

Or make a right onto a dirt road at the town hall, and proceed about one-half mile to your first left, another dirt road that heads uphill.

Follow this until you reach an electric fence across the road marking the entrance to the Barr Hill Nature Preserve, managed by the Vermont Nature Conservancy.

Continuing up the old road, you will see a pull-out and trail on the left, which lead to panoramic views of the lake and surrounding historic landscape from the top of Barr Hill. (From the town hall to the top of Barr Hill and back is about 4 miles.)

Guildhall

*T*HE VILLAGE OF GUILDHALL, laid out in a wide Connecticut River meadow, wears its responsibility as shire town of Essex County in an understated way. Wild strawberries grow on the green. Facing it, a plain white courthouse and a plain white church stand side by side. A sign claims this to be the only town in the world so named and, further, that it is pronounced "Gilhall."

Guildhall was the first settlement in the wilderness that was Essex County in 1764. In 1776 a block-house was built on the river to guard against attack from that watery highway. In 1802 the town was chosen county seat of what is still the least populated, most densely forested county in Vermont. Farming the fertile river plain and logging the forests have been the chief occupations of residents, although at various times the village had a sawmill and gristmill, taverns, a wool-carding mill, and a harness and saddle factory.

With tranquil dignity, Guildhall goes about its business in buildings dating back to the early days. At first glance it is hard to tell which of the two white buildings at the head of the green is a church and which a courthouse. Both are small, unadorned, white clapboard structures with two-tier bell towers.

The church, built in 1844, has green shutters and double doors. The county courthouse, built in 1850 to replace one built in 1802, is capped by a weather-vane. The recently restored courtroom, with its origi-nal wide-plank floors, brass lighting fixtures, and spindle-back wooden benches, seems to be the essence of a place where simple justice can be found.

Behind the courthouse the county grammar school (1805) is now the office of the county extension service. Opposite the green is a library and Masonic hall (1900) with a circular belfry bound by columns. The oldest building, dating from 1795, is the Guild Hall on the southeast corner of the green. Over the years it has been lawyers' and doctors' offices, a bank, a harness shop, and a store. It became a community center and the town offices in 1920 when residents joined another small building to the original.

On the broad Connecticut River plain around the village are fields and pasture farmed since the first settlers arrived. Some farms have the extended architecture of an attached house and barn often seen in northern New England. Forested hills surround the farmlands and now cover most of the town, as well as most of Essex County. Much of the forestland is owned by paper companies and is managed to encourage and maintain production. If Vermont still has a frontier, this is it.

With tranquil dignity, Guildhall goes about its business
in buildings dating back to the early days. The oldest building, dating from 1795,
is the Guild Hall on the southwest corner of the green.

BEGIN YOUR WALK on the green in Guildhall village. Explore the buildings around it, and then proceed 1.2 miles west on Vermont Route 102 to North Road. Here, turn right and walk a mile or so to get a feeling for the countryside. Return to the village along the same route, taking in views of the White Mountains in New Hampshire to the east.

Highgate

*T*HE FARMING VILLAGES of Highgate Center and Highgate Falls lie on opposite high banks of the Missisquoi River. These clusters of buildings—the churches, the houses, a feed store, the markets—sit like an island in a plateau of fields and pasture. Replacing an old iron bridge intended for people and horses, a wide new highway bridge designed for speed now connects the two villages. But in effect the new bridge divides the villages, only a half mile apart, in a way they have never been before. It's now quicker to cross by car but risky on foot.

The first people came to this area shortly after the glaciers retreated some 10,000 years ago, and for thousands of years the Missisquoi was their water trail through the forests. The Abenakis settled along its shores, hunted the woods, and fished the river. Their descendants, long woven into other ethnic strains, share a fierce pride in their Native American heritage and struggle to maintain it. Many live in this corner of Vermont.

The Town of Highgate was issued a charter and a name by Governor Benning Wentworth of New Hampshire in 1763. The first permanent white settlers in 1785 were former Hessian soldiers, who may have thought they were settling in Canada. Despite border questions, they stayed and around 1791 chose officers to organize the town.

Highgate Falls has a surprisingly long green stretching between facing rows of lofty maple trees. At the river end is an example of elegance from around 1870, a brick mansion painted a rich yellow with elaborate white carved wood trim and a mansard roof that flares like a bell. At the other end of the green stands the brick St. John's Episcopal Church, built around 1831 by congregations from several religious denominations, who then shared the church.

In Highgate Center a stone Civil War soldier stands sentry over the green with its benches and picnic tables. To the east is the 1886 brick Methodist church with decorative trim highlighting its round-top windows and a wooden three-tier steeple. A red frame house nearby has a recessed second-story porch overlooking the main street like a small stage. The Oddfellows' Hall occupies an imposing brick building and is prominently marked "Gentlemens Club."

Between the villages is the site of the great falls of the Missisquoi, where the river drops more than 75 feet. Dammed at an early date, the falls provided power for a sawmill, a gristmill, and later a foundry and machine shops. The old 1878 iron bridge, a rare lenticular truss type, still spans the falls, awaiting rehabilitation for use as a footbridge.

Surrounding the villages is some of the best farmland in the state. Dairy farms stretch as far as the eye can see.

The first people came to this area shortly after the glaciers retreated some 10,000 years ago, and for thousands of years the Missisquoi was their water trail through the forests.

BEGIN YOUR WALK on Vermont Route 78 at the green in Highgate Center, and explore the village.

A road heads south from the green and leads in two-tenths of a mile to the Missisquoi River and the iron bridge.

For a look at the countryside, head northwest from the green on St. Armand Road for a mile or so, as you like, and return.

You can reach Highgate Falls in a half-mile by heading west from the Highgate Center green on Route 78 and then turning left (south) on Vermont Route 207. If there is traffic when you cross the new highway bridge, you may wish you had taken your car for this side-trip. The bridge is narrow and has no sidewalks.

Hyde Park

*H*YDE PARK'S MAIN BUSINESS is justice on a small scale. This village, one of the smallest in Lamoille County, is nonetheless the county seat. At one end of Main Street the defender general's office works out of an old frame house with an attached barn. At the other end the justice of the peace has a cozy cottage with a front porch. In between, the red brick courthouse presides.

In 1836, when it was tapped as the site of the newly formed county and its court, Hyde Park was a small farm village built along an east-west road following the banks of the Lamoille River. Soon lawyers, inn-keepers, and a printer joined the suppliers of goods and services for surrounding farms. After the Civil War a calfskin tannery became not only the most prosperous business in town but briefly the largest in the world. In 1910 a fire swept through the western portion of the village, and new buildings soon replaced those lost.

Nearly all of Hyde Park was built between 1836 and about 1915. Houses on Church Street and Commonwealth Avenue are festooned with the then popular wooden ornaments cut by the scroll saw. On Main Street the white Page mansion with multiple chimneys and a wing at an oblique angle was the home of the tannery owner. It was the only building in that area to escape the 1910 fire, allegedly because most of the available water was directed at it, since its owner was by then a U.S. senator. Buildings erected after the fire include the imposing brick courthouse with its clock tower, the diminutive but grandly named opera house (still presenting live entertainment), and the buff-colored brick public library.

Bypassed by the main highway to the north, Hyde Park has been spared much modern traffic. Woods and fields start at the village fringe and roll up foothills to where some of the highest peaks of the Green Mountains are visible beyond. Nearby on the Lamoille River are powerful Cadys Falls, long harnessed for power. As you walk up the steep river bluff from the Lamoille and arrive in peaceful Hyde Park, you will be surprised that slow-moving cars rather than wagons pass you on the way.

Nearly all of Hyde Park was built between 1836 and about 1915.
Many houses are festooned with the then popular wooden ornaments cut by the scroll saw.

BEGIN YOUR WALK in the village at the courthouse, head east on Main Street, and as the road divides at the high school, veer right down to the river floodplain.

Cross the narrow bridge, continue straight across the floodplain about a mile, cross the river at Cadys Falls, and as you begin uphill, bear right.

For the next mile this road will pass through a working farm landscape with Mount Mansfield visible ahead before you arrive at Morristown Corners, where there is a general store and a used book shop in an old, rambling brick house.

Return to Hyde Park by the same route. (Hyde Park to Morristown Corners and return, about 5 miles.)

Isle La Motte

$\mathcal{N}$OW FOR SOMEPLACE completely different. Water, not mountains or forest, defines the landscape of Isle La Motte, the smallest of the three islands in Lake Champlain that, together with a small peninsula, make up Grand Isle County. Its flat fields barely rise above the lake. And the dominant color is the blue of water and sky instead of the green so associated with the rest of Vermont.

Isle La Motte, reached by a causeway, is the site of the first white settlement in Vermont. A French regiment commanded by Captain Pierre de La Motte built Fort St. Anne on its western shore in 1666 to protect lands claimed by the French from incursion by the Mohawks. In the chapel of this wilderness fort, Jesuits held the first mass in what became Vermont. But the outpost was abandoned the next year after many of its occupants fell ill and died during the long winter. The Shrine of St. Anne is now on the site, with services held daily in an outdoor chapel from May to October.

The Isle has also been a part of many other chapters in Lake Champlain history. It is thought Samuel de Champlain landed here in 1609 when he first explored the lake. In 1776 Benedict Arnold anchored his fleet offshore before the battle of Valcour Island in the American Revolution. In the War of 1812 the British secured an anchorage offshore from which they sailed to meet the Americans at the Battle of Plattsburgh. During much of the 19th and early 20th centuries, quarries on Isle La Motte produced limestone and marble used in many lakeshore buildings, as well as the Vermont State House and even Rockefeller Center in New York City. Vice-President Theodore Roosevelt happened to be on this remote island in September 1901 when he received word that President William McKinley had been shot.

Today on Isle La Motte it seems as if nothing has happened for quite a while. There are still a number of farms with historic houses and barns, and apple orchards have long been part of the scene, as on the other islands. The center is a tiny hamlet sitting in this landscape of open fields and hedgerows. A house and the town library there are built of the large gray limestone blocks that were quarried on the island. Aside from crowds on Sundays at the Shrine, the island is quiet and sparsely populated. There is no store or restaurant, except for the seasonal cafeteria at the Shrine. Relatively unknown to tourists, the island is now mostly a place to bicycle, walk, or fish.

Aside from crowds on Sundays at the Shrine, the island is quiet and sparsely populated. Relatively unknown to tourists, the island is now mostly a place to bicycle, walk, or fish.

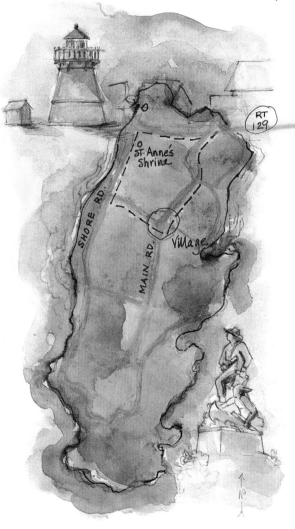

BEGIN YOUR WALK near the stone town library on The Main Road in the hamlet of Isle La Motte.

Head west a little over a mile to the lake, and turn right and head north along Shore Road, where you will see the silos of farms across the lake in New York.

At St. Anne's Shrine, an oversized statue of Samuel de Champlain gazes out over the lake, and there is the outdoor chapel and cafeteria, with a small beach and picnic tables nearby. A short detour north from the Shrine on Lighthouse Road will allow you to glimpse the former Isle La Motte Lighthouse, now painted pink.

Head east from the Shrine along Shrine Road until you reach The Main Road, and then head south back to the hamlet and your starting point. (Loop from library to the shrine and back is about 5.5 miles.)

Johnson

*U*NTIL THE 1980s Johnson had a soda fountain serving nickel ice cream cones. It's gone now, but an aura of that past clings to the village. The buildings along its wide central street are trimmed in styles popular in the mid-19th century, when the local woolen mill and sawmill were booming. Many now have new uses, including as studios and living quarters for artists of the Vermont Studio Center. When it was established in 1984, the center picked up a thread in Johnson's history from 50 years before, when several artists were drawn to the area by the hilly pastoral scenes that surround the village.

In the 1780s settlers from New Hampshire first cleared the wilderness that was Johnson for small farms along the wide, fertile Lamoille River floodplain. They soon discovered the power potential of waterfalls on the nearby Gihon River. The village of Johnson grew around a gristmill and a woolen mill erected along the falls. In the 1850s the village became an education center when residents erected the county grammar school, which evolved into a teacher's college in 1867. In the late 19th century the railroad came and went, leaving Railroad Street behind. Johnson Woolen Mill, the scaled-down successor to the original, no longer spins and weaves but still makes wool hunting pants and jackets so thick it seems they could stand on their own.

Over the bridge below the Gihon River falls stands a rambling former gristmill, now the administrative center of the Studio Center. Along Main Street the center has revived deteriorating and underused buildings. The original grammar school, Chesamore Hall, has a white roof crown and decorative eave brackets that date from an expansion in the teachers' college. The Town Hall and Opera House, now lecture and studio space, retains its plain meeting house facade from when it was the village's original Congregational church of 1832. The Baptist church (1855) is now the Masonic Hall, but its clock facing Main Street belongs to the town, a gift during the transfer.

Johnson lies on the sloping eastern shoulder of the Green Mountains, the glacier-shaped remnants of the oldest mountains in New England. The village grew among their foothills on the flat land of the Lamoille River Valley, a strip still important for dairy farming. A walk from the village along the dirt road curving beside the broad river passes farm fields cleared from the water's edge to a steep wooded hillside. A sawmill along the route turns logs to lumber, and the trucks rumbling through town carrying bundles of massive logs on their backs are a reminder that forests still fuel the local economy.

In the 1780s settlers from New Hampshire first cleared the wilderness
that was Johnson for small farms along the wide, fertile Lamoille River floodplain,
a strip still important for dairy farming.

o Johnson State College

RT 15

Village

RT 15

PATCH RD.

LAMOILLE RIVER

→ farms

BEGIN YOUR WALK on Main Street (Vermont Route 15) and explore the village. (The street that heads north from the town hall crosses the Gihon River and passes the former grist- mill on its way to Johnson State College.)

Starting at the town hall, head west on Main Street to Railroad Street, turn left, and head south to the steel truss bridge over the Lamoille River.

After you cross the river, turn left on the dirt road that runs through the sawmill (Patch Road) and walk for a little over a mile into farmland.

Return to Main Street by the same route. (From Main Street and Railroad Street out Patch Road to the farms and return: about 3.2 miles.)

St. Johnsbury

A VISITOR WALKING through the gracious 19th-century streets of 20th-century St. Johnsbury may well ask, How did all this happen and how have they managed to keep it? This rather remote small city has a natural history museum and planetarium guarded by stone lions. It has a public library with spiral stairways, gleaming carved black walnut and oak paneling and, tucked in back, is the oldest unaltered art gallery in the country, with a wall-sized painting by Albert Bierstadt.

It all happened because the native Fairbanks family, inventors of the platform scale in 1830, built their factory here, brought prosperity to the town, and shared their fortune by building the museum, library, and churches, among other buildings. And it remains one of Vermont's most architecturally significant urban townscapes.

As the Fairbanks scale factory boomed, St. Johnsbury became the county seat in 1856, and it thrived as a manufacturing center into the mid-20th century.

Main Street lies on a plateau that is the stage for the prominent public buildings and high-style houses, united by small parks at each end (at St. Johnsbury Academy and at Mount Pleasant Street). The St. Johnsbury House, an 1850 hotel at the halfway point, was saved from demolition in the 1970s by a public effort that recognized that it was too important a part of this magnificent street to lose.

Many buildings along Main Street were designed by local architect Lambert Packard, whose work encompasses all the major styles popular between the late 1800s and 1920. He designed the St. Johnsbury Athenaeum (1871), a public library with the atmosphere of a private sanctuary, and the Fairbanks Museum of Natural Science (1891), which visitors enter through massive sandstone arches. Both are worth seeing inside and out.

Further down the street several churches make an interesting contrast. There is the simplicity of the classical, painted wood frame South Congregational (1842, rebuilt 1852) and Packard's robust rusticated limestone North Congregational (1891) with a five-story tower thrusting heavenward. A detour downhill on Eastern Avenue passes an eight-sided brick house (1854) and the former post office in its new guise as an arts center. On Railroad Street the commercial and railroad district of well-kept red brick buildings is doing business in its second century.

A few farms persist around the village, despite the short growing season and rocky hills, and much land has been overtaken by the northern forest. As you walk, however, a view of the patchwork of fields and woods now and then unfolds like a map across a valley to the hills beyond.

As the Fairbanks scale factory boomed, St. Johnsbury became the county seat in 1856, and it thrived as a manufacturing center into the mid-20th century.

BEGIN YOUR WALK, after exploring Main Street, on Mount Pleasant Street (Mount Pleasant Street intersects Main Street four blocks northeast of the Fairbanks Museum).

Walk uphill past a yellow octagonal house (1876), veer right onto Mount Pleasant Street Extension, and pass the Mount Pleasant Cemetery.

The road turns to dirt and there are good views across the Passumpsic River Valley.

After nearly a mile, the road goes under Interstate 91 and then overlooks the fields of the Sleepers River Valley.

Return by the same route. (From the corner of Main Street and Mount Pleasant Street out to the Sleepers Valley overlook and return is about 3.5 miles.)

Shelburne

SHELBURNE, WITH A MUSEUM VILLAGE of Americana and a semi-public 1,000-acre estate on Lake Champlain, is no ordinary town. Although it is essentially suburban today and attracts many summer and fall tourists, it also retains a 19th-century village around a green where the houses and shops would still be familiar to the residents from that time. Only the uses have changed.

Shelburne, chartered in 1763, had ten families prior to the Revolution and by 1785 a sawmill and forge at the falls on the La Platte River. During the War of 1812 boats seized by the Americans were brought to the Shelburne Bay shipyard to be outfitted as fighting vessels. The shipyard continued to play an important role in Lake Champlain history, launching the first steamer in 1825 as well as the last sidewheeler in 1905. Meanwhile life elsewhere in the town revolved around the seasonal rhythms of farming, like most other Champlain Valley towns. In the 1880s William Seward and Lila Vanderbilt Webb acquired more than 30 small farms to form Shelburne Farms, a model 3,800-acre agricultural estate on Lake Champlain that was later divided between their two sons. On the south end of the village, Electra Havemeyer Webb in 1947 founded the Shelburne Museum, a collection of representative historic American structures moved to the site and filled to overflowing with Americana.

In the village a large white clapboard tavern-inn from 1796 (now an inn-motel) stands at the north end of the triangular green. Facing one another across the green are a mid-19th-century brick commercial block and a rambling, red, wood frame country store built in 1859. Nearby is the painted brick library with its classical portico that was added in 1911 to the front of a house built in 1815. At the south end of the green stand the stone Methodist church (1873) and the Catholic church (1895). (The Catholic church's small frame parish house was originally a chapel at Shelburne Farms for servants on the estate.) On U.S. 7 north of the green, the Episcopal church is constructed of Monkton dolomite, quarried locally and known as redstone.

With the lake and bay as its borders, much of Shelburne is a landscape of gentle rolling hills with a patchwork of meadows and woods, increasingly dotted with new development. However, there are still three dairy farms and an orchard, as well as agricultural activities at Shelburne Farms, where a Brown Swiss herd provides milk for the farm's famous cheese. This estate, the largest in New England, was saved from piecemeal development by conversion to nonprofit status and tax arrangements made with the town, which successfully preserved both the estate and much of the town's pastoral character. With the growing city of Burlington to the north and U.S. Route 7 passing through the village, Shelburne residents continue to face the task of balancing a rural past with the demands for commercial and residential development in the future.

Although it is essentially suburban today, it also retains a 19th-century village around a green where the houses and shops would still be familiar to the residents from that time.

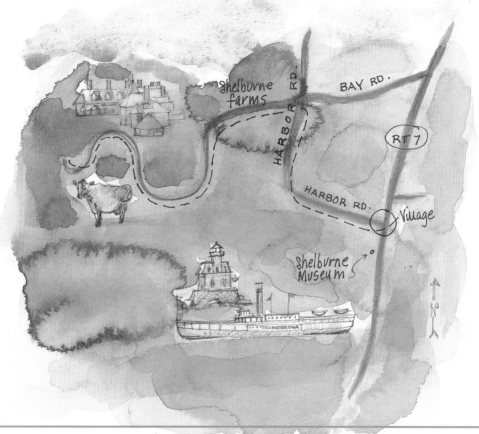

BEGIN YOUR WALK at the green and explore the village. Cross U.S. Route 7 at the stoplight, and head west on Harbor Road 1.8 miles

to Shelburne Farms. Caution, traffic on Harbor Road can be heavy. At the farm entrance you can get directions for a walk

through meadows and woods past the mammoth turreted, half-timbered Farm Barn to Lone Tree Point (3 miles round-trip).

Return to the village along the same route on Harbor Road. (From the village to Shelburne Farms entrance and return: about 3.6 miles.)

Stowe

STOWE IS THE MOUNTAIN TOWN that was swallowed by a resort. But it's still there in the little Main Street houses with Victorian filigree now converted to shops and in the farmhouses turned ski lodges. It's also in the services it continues to provide to a rural community. While glitz is available, Stowe seems to be a town that has learned to play in the big leagues of skiing, tourism, and second homes without losing itself. As development creeps up the mountain road, Stowe's sense of place endures because the 19th-century village is essentially intact.

Settled in 1794, Stowe was named for a town in England, with the "e" added later. On its western side it includes 4,393-foot Mount Mansfield, the highest point in Vermont. The village grew in the valley between the Green Mountains and the Worcester Range, where the Little River meets the West Branch. A sawmill and gristmill were in place by 1796, and wood products businesses, such as a maker of wooden bowls, continue today. Dairy farming has diminished and been pushed further from the village but still contributes to the life of the area.

History reports women and men climbing Mount Mansfield in the early 19th century. Tourism followed. In 1850 the big brick house, which is now the Green Mountain Inn, was converted for guests, and soon there was a trail to ride horseback to the mountaintop. Tapping a vogue for vacationing in luxury on mountaintops, a 200-room hotel with large livery barns was perched on the summit in 1864 but burned in 1889. Skiing began in the 1930s on logging roads, then on trails cut by the Civilian Conservation Corps. Since 1940, when the longest chair lift in the country took off up the mountain, Stowe has been coping with its success.

Village buildings retain much of their character in a range of 19th-century architectural styles. Shops in houses set back on lawns still relate to each other and the street in a residential way. The white-columned Community Church's unusually lofty steeple looks down a short street to the white frame former high school, which is now the library and art center. One of the first residences to host early skiers is the rambling white house with black shutters, now an inn, beyond the covered foot bridge at the bottom of the Mountain Road.

Country walkers have an opportunity to try one of the earliest pedestrian paths in the country's growing greenways movement. Leading through the countryside from behind the Community Church, the paved Stowe Recreation Path winds gradually up the mountain through the town's woodsy backyard. It crisscrosses the river on arched wooden foot bridges and rambles past farm fields and through woodlands over private property obtained by donation or easement in the spirit of common access to nature. It has become a linear village green mingling walkers of all ages, runners, infants in strollers, bicyclists, and even cross-country skiers.

Stowe's sense of place endures because the 19th-century village is essentially intact. It's still there in the little houses with Victorian filigree now converted to shops and in the farmhouses turned ski lodges

BEGIN YOUR WALK on Vermont Route 100 in the center of town and explore the village.

Then find the tall steeple of the Community Church and behind it access one end of the Stowe Recreation Path.

The path is 5.3 end to end, so make your walk as long or short as you wish.

Brookfield

O F ALL THE VERMONT VILLAGES time seems to have forgotten, the upland village of Brookfield is distinctive. No other has a bridge like this. Driving on Vermont Route 65 from the west road into town, you see a mirror-like lake ahead, and what seem to be planks lying on the water to get you to the other side. Water squirts through the planks as a car moves between fencelike guardrails over the single lane supported by 380 pontoons. Although this adventure is a surprise in this out-of-the-way place, a pontoon bridge has been here since 1820, when the first was laid over Sunset Lake by a few neighbors. This rare bridge is the seventh, built in 1978. On summer days fishermen on the bridge have a line in the placid water. Catches are limited to "5 trout or 5 pounds."

Brookfield is a sleepy spot with tall trees shading the gravel main street. Paved roads end at the village as if to say, "That was now, this is then," and white clapboard 19th-century buildings nourish the impression of time reversing. The village grew in a linear way on a plateau along the Montpelier-to-Randolph Stage Road, once a main north-south route. The public library, founded in 1791 and now in a former residence, is the oldest continuing library in the state.

Quiet as it is today, Brookfield bustled once as it harnessed the energy of Sunset Brook, which flows into the long, narrow lake. Thirteen mills turned out agricultural tools and other products. Once a pitch-fork factory, Wilder House, a low building with a cupola at the end of the bridge, is the last industrial remnant of that era. The dam is still there, but now the lake shore is grassy or wooded.

Along the single street the former town hall, once a center of community activities, is a large three-story structure with double doors and three rows of large windows. On a rise across the street at the library and town clerk's office hangs a bulletin board of village goings-on: recycling projects, garden club meetings, auctions, lost dogs, free kittens. Next door, a group of former residences is now an inn. Just beyond is Brookfield's most architecturally significant house, distinguished by a wide, recessed, arched balcony with ornate railing and a front entrance flanked by fluted columns. Beyond the south edge of the village rises the thin steeple of the First Congregational Church (1846), distinguished by a high-columned portico.

Brookfield village lies on a ridge, and not far to the west Interstate 89 cuts through a landscape of forests and meadows, a rare modern intrusion. Further west the outline of the Green Mountains dominates the horizon. To the east are wooded, hilly uplands, dominated by the northern New England hardwoods—maple, birch, and beech—whose vivid reds and yellows glow against dark spruce, hemlock, and pine in the fall.

Brookfield is a sleepy spot with tall trees shading the gravel main street.
The village grew in a linear way on a plateau along the Montpelier-to-Randolph Stage Road,
once a main north-south route.

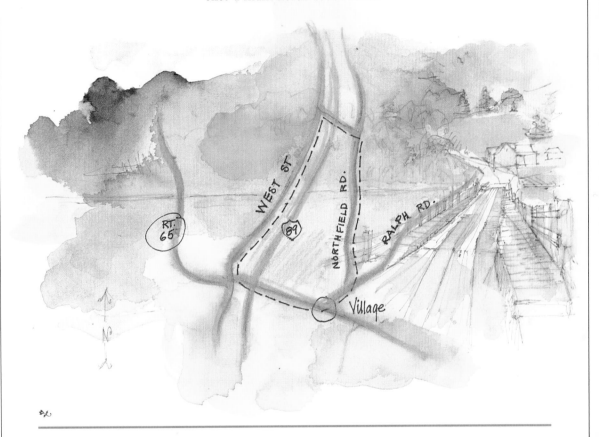

BEGIN YOUR WALK at the floating bridge near the old pitchfork factory. Head north along the main street (Northfield Road) out of the village.

Continue almost a mile and turn left on the road going under the Interstate. Then turn left again onto West Street and head south.

Just past North Pond on your right, turn left yet again onto Vermont Route 65, and cross over the Interstate and then

the floating bridge back to your starting point. (Round-trip: 2.8 miles.)

Chelsea

CHELSEA KNOWS HOW to separate church and state. In the middle of this quiet little farming community, the white church and the county courthouse each sit on its own green. Houses and commercial buildings from the same era, the mid-19th century, surround them. All are aging gracefully, and their size and refinement reflect Chelsea's lively past. The scene typifies an ideal American village-scape, now being copied by designers elsewhere, but here it is simply town history.

In 1784 Chelsea was settled by southern New Englanders, as was most of Vermont. They pushed north to found the town along the First Branch of the White River. Farms were soon cleared from forest on the surrounding hills. In 1794 it was made the shire town for Orange County, and the county court sessions brought lawyers, judges, sheriffs, and jurors to the increasingly active village. Chelsea also embraced a mix of farmers and merchants, creating its own bank and a range of shops and services. It became the center for a thriving community of hill farms in the early 19th century when sheep farming was popular, a role that continued through the century as dairying became the agricultural specialty.

Chelsea's buildings cluster along the main street and the two greens, converted over the centuries to new uses as needed. Not only are there twin greens, but the most prominent commercial buildings are a matched pair of brick stores from the early 1800s in a formal style more common to urban settings. The one on the right is in original condition, with irregular bricks in a mellow orange-red; the other was rebuilt in 1927 but retains its original plan.

At the head of the first green stands the white frame United Church of Chelsea (1813, renovated in 1848), whose clock tower is topped by a belfry weathervane sweeping the sky. On the second green the county courthouse (1847), with its own tower and belfry and orderly rows of windows with shutters, also follows the form of a traditional New England church. The school is next door, and the village cemetery is behind it on a hill with a view of the valley.

This high plateau, southeast of the foothills of the Green Mountains, is the place where the First Branch of the White River gently meanders through heavily wooded hills. Although the area has one of the state's shortest growing seasons (just 111 days), farming continues on a small scale, enough to domesticate the landscape with an occasional meadow or pasture. Many abandoned hill farms have returned the hillsides to forest, and the pastures are closer to the valley. Tourism and recreation never developed in this region, which remains somewhat remote even now, bypassed by the Interstate. This makes it all the more inviting for a quiet walk in a classic village and through the deep woods nearby.

Not only are there twin greens, but the most prominent commercial buildings are a matched pair of brick stores from the early 1800s in a formal style more common to urban settings.

BEGIN YOUR WALK at the Chelsea greens and explore the village. Then near the church on the northern green, head uphill (east) on Vermont Route 113 a little over three-quarters of a mile,

and make the first right onto the dirt Town Farm Road.

Head south on this high road through dense woods for 2 miles down to a T intersection with

Cotton Brook Road and make a right.

Go a short distance, turn right again and then stay right again onto the Old Strafford Road, which follows Jenkins

Brook out to the paved Vermont Route 110.

At 110 turn right and head north back into the village with its twin stores and twin greens. (Round-trip: 6.5 miles.)

East Barnard

THE HAMLET OF EAST BARNARD lies along an unpaved road deep in the countryside. It is so quiet that the brook flowing behind the few houses makes the loudest sound, and then only in spring as the melting snow runs off the surrounding high, hilly land. It seems miles from anywhere, certainly from any paved roads. That, of course, is the point. People often move to this area to escape the buzz of modern life. In the 1930s journalist Dorothy Thompson and her husband, novelist Sinclair Lewis, were among them.

Originally, though, the town of Barnard, settled in 1775, was a prosperous farming community whose villages supplied its commercial and social needs. The first farms in Vermont were on hillsides, which were dry and easier to clear than the wetlands in the valleys. Later, after the lowlands were cleared, hill farms declined. The town of Barnard had nearly 2,000 people in 1830 but soon began losing them to opportunities elsewhere. It was a common story in Vermont; people were among its largest exports well into the 20th century. The farms that remained in Barnard often absorbed some of the smaller farms, and these new, larger farms turned to dairying.

Perhaps the most distinctive house in East Barnard village is an early brick story-and-a-half residence with three chimneys. It was built around 1830 as a tavern and on the upper story has a dance floor with stenciled walls. Several years later Methodists erected the wood frame church and allowed other denominations to use it in proportion to their numbers. Its front windows may seem oddly placed but are explained by the fact that the church was designed for two entrances and built with only one. Not far is the old two-story district school with a louvered belfry. The building is now used as a residence.

Every road out of the village passes through undeveloped forest land. The Amity Pond natural area is to the east. To the west is Hawks Hill, a new conservation area managed by the Vermont Nature Conservancy. And there are still a few farms that have cleared pastures and gardens among the trees. Although Woodstock and ski areas are nearby and the former Thompson-Lewis house is now a luxury inn, the modern scene seems a long way from East Barnard.

It is so quiet that the brook flowing behind the few houses makes the loudest sound.
It seems miles from anywhere, certainly from any paved roads.
That, of course, is the point.

BEGIN YOUR WALK by the old Methodist church.

After exploring the village, head from the church up the East Barnard Road.

This road makes a slow switchback uphill for a little over 2 miles before arriving at the Amity Pond Waterfowl Area on the right.

Here at your leisure follow the many trails through brooks, wetlands, woods, and meadows.

Return to East Barnard by the same route. (From the church to the Amity Pond area entrance and return: 4.5 miles.)

Middlebury

*M*IDDLEBURY IS A COLLEGE TOWN thriving after two centuries not only as a cultural center but a center of services for many villages and farms in the surrounding Champlain Valley. Its substantial white clapboard and mellow brick houses speak of a gracious past prosperity, while the bustle of traffic skirting the central green indicates a lively present.

Situated in the broadest part of the valley lowlands between the Green Mountains and Lake Champlain, this site appealed to early settlers in the 1770s as relatively flat, rich farmland. Otter Creek bisects it, cutting through the glacial layer of clay, sand, and broken stone that covers most of Vermont down to bedrock. Where the river tumbles over one rocky set of waterfalls, settlers built a sawmill in 1774, which in the next century became the humming industrial area along Mill Street. John Deere, a blacksmith, learned his trade here before heading west to invent the steel plow.

In 1802 the first marble finishing mill in the United States opened here, and the village remained a center of stone finishing off and on well into the 20th century. Outcrops of marble can still be spotted along the river below the falls, and the finished product can be seen as the trim and foundations on houses and in the Marbleworks group of sparkling white marble buildings overlooking the falls. Nearby, the arches of the marble Main Street bridge (1892) are modeled on the grander Pont Sant'Angelo in Rome. Middlebury College (founded in 1800), with its campus built in gray limestone and marble, is another expression of the importance of the local stone finishing industry.

The Middlebury green, however, is still the center of the village, presided over by the striking white Congregational church (1806-1809), with its graceful five-tiered steeple, each varied layer diminishing in size as it reaches heavenward. It is considered the masterpiece of Lavius Fillmore, a house joiner who is also thought responsible for the stone Episcopal church on the green, an unusually early (1826) use of Gothic Revival style.

Among the many fine 19th-century houses in the village are a number you can enter since their conversion to public uses: the Sheldon Museum, the Painter House (now the Vermont Folklife Center), the Swift House Inn, and the John Warren House. The Middlebury Inn on the green, although altered inside, has the same fanlit doorway and red brick facade that have welcomed guests since 1827.

As you leave the village and walk into the countryside, you will see a landscape of small farms with woodlots, orchards, and rolling fields with islands of shade trees. If you look back, you will see the village spires and dove-gray college buildings set off against the Green Mountains (brilliant in fall). From such a vantage this village seems remote in a rural stillness that transcends today.

The Middlebury green is still the center of the village,
presided over by the striking white Congregational church (1806-1809).

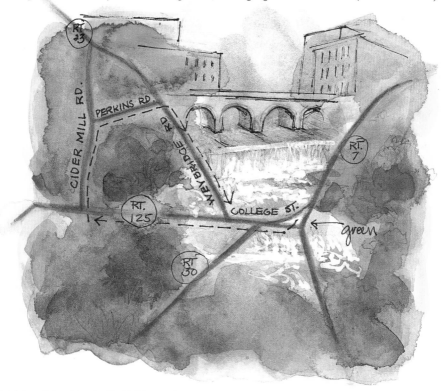

BEGIN YOUR WALK at the green and explore the village. Don't miss the area below the falls on Mill Street, where you can cross the river on a footbridge and rest on wooden benches nearby.

Then head west on the combined Vermont Routes 30, 125, and 23 (Main Street). In two blocks, veer right and follow College Street (Route 125) past Middlebury College and out of the village.

Walk over a mile and a half and make your first right onto Cider Mill Road. Continue over a mile and take your first right onto Perkins Road. Proceed less than a mile to the T intersection with paved Route 23

(Weybridge Road), and turn right.

A walk of little over a mile with fine views will bring you back to an intersection with College Street in the village. (This loop, round-trip, is a little over 6 miles.)

Montpelier

*W*ITH ONLY 9,000 PEOPLE, Montpelier, the nation's smallest state capital, seems rightly paired with the most rural state in the country. It wears its golden dome with dignity, but with a homey, approachable, small-town attitude. There is no governor's mansion; he or she continues to live at home. The big front yard of the Vermont State House doubles as a green for both the city and the state.

Montpelier was settled in 1788 at the junction of the Winooski River and its North Branch. It became the state capital in 1805, chosen because it is near the center of the state (and its citizens pledged $8,000 toward building a state house). The first State House (1808) was replaced in 1838 by a second, which burned in 1858, leaving its granite columns and portico to be incorporated into the third State House (1859), the one that stands today.

Well situated at the junction of rivers and roads, Montpelier was and is more than just the capital. A commercial and manufacturing center, it boasted a woolen mill, many woodworking shops, and, with the world's largest granite quarries within a few miles, many shops and services for that industry. Today National Life insurance company is the largest private employer. In this century the city has suffered two destructive floods, in November 1927 and March 1992.

Any visit to Montpelier should begin with the Vermont State House, whose monumental portico is modeled after the Temple of Theseus in Athens. Atop its gleaming gold dome stands a wooden statue of Ceres, the goddess of agriculture, carved by the sergeant-at-arms in 1938.

Down the street, the red brick Pavilion Building, with fancy two-story porches, an apparently full-blown Victorian-era structure, is actually a replica of the 1876 Pavilion Hotel, where generations of legislators stayed. Rebuilt in the 1960s, it now houses state offices and the Vermont Historical Society. State offices have also wisely been tucked into the many old residences along State and Baldwin streets, maintaining the streetscape and look of an earlier time.

Downtown, at the corner of State and Main streets, delightfully varied rows of commercial buildings typical of the late 19th century stretch north, south, and west. Upper Main Street has a number of mansions from both the early and late 1800s. And in the surrounding neighborhoods, Montpelier's hills mean that streets often slant, and houses are built on many levels.

The countryside is close, even within the city. Behind the State House, a forested hill laced with old carriage roads and trails forms Hubbard Park, which is accessed by steep residential streets that give way to the tranquility of dirt roads and the greenery of the park. Inside and outside Montpelier, there is a lot to be found within a small space.

The city wears its golden dome with dignity, but with
a homey, approachable, small-town attitude. There is no governor's mansion.
The big front yard of the State House doubles as a green for the city and the state.

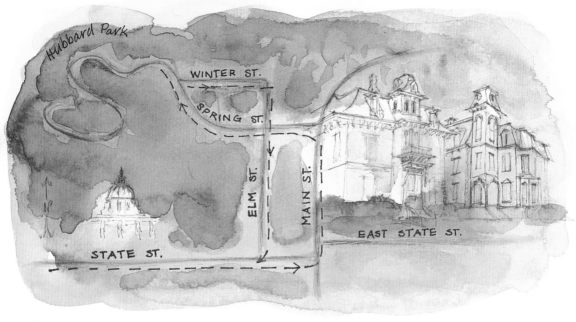

BEGIN YOUR WALK at the State House and proceed east past the Pavilion Building down State Street toward downtown. At the stoplight at State and Main, head north along upper Main Street, past the many 19th-century mansions.

At the T where Main Street goes to the right, turn left onto Spring Street, cross Elm Street, and across the next corner (with Summer Street) follow the paved road uphill to the gate of Hubbard Park.

After you wander the park at your leisure, find your way back to the entrance and, as you descend, keep to the left to drop down Winter Street and cross Summer Street to again reach Elm Street.

Turn right, and walk down Elm all the way back to State Street, where a turn to the right will bring you back to the State House. (Round-trip to the gate of Hubbard Park: approximately 2 miles.)

Newbury

NEWBURY is a Connecticut River village that looks much as it did in its prime, the first half of the 19th century. Its white buildings follow a linear pattern as many villages along the river do, but it is still a safe flood distance above the river lowlands. The river, which served as a highway for settlers before the Revolution, sweeps behind it in a dramatic curve, defining the fertile fields of what is called the Great Oxbow.

The village quietly minds its business around a broad green with a large memorial marker to General Jacob Bayley. He settled the town in 1763 and during the Revolution, with Moses Hazen, cleared the Bayley-Hazen Military Road, which began in Wells River in the northeast corner of town. Along the rear of the green, the Village Hall, the school, and the Methodist church stand in a row. Across from the green is the general store, as much a pulse of town activity as the neighboring town hall, post office, bank, library, and churches. At noon the carillon in the Second Congregational Church is likely to ring out "A Mighty Fortress Is Our God" over the peaceful scene.

Much of Newbury bears the classic, white lines of the Greek Revival, the style popular during the village's period of greatest growth, 1835 to 1860. Some of the Greek Revival houses are built onto the front of earlier dwellings from the frontier era. And the white clapboard houses built after a disastrous fire in 1913 match the earlier style. Victorian variations in the otherwise white village streetscape are the red

brick library (1896), with a massive stone entrance arch, and the tiny brick bank (1884), with gilt letters spelling "BANK" in a fanlight over the door.

Newbury has the wide river at its feet and a modest mountain at its back.

Mount Pulaski offers a spectacular view over the village green to the Great Oxbow of the river, with the peaks of the White Mountains visible beyond. From here it is easy to see the appeal of the rich river bottomland to the first white settlers (especially since the Abenaki had already cleared the oxbow for their lodges and corn hills). The original survey of the town in 1763 divided it into meadow lots on the river for farming, house lots on the river road (now Main Street), and larger lots in the wooded hills. That plan remains largely visible today, and the tempo of the early farming village remains.

The village quietly minds its business around a broad green
with a large memorial marker to General Jacob Bayley.
He settled the town in 1763 and cleared the Bayley-Hazen Military Road.

BEGIN YOUR WALK at the green, then head north along Main Street (U.S. Route 5). Cross the bridge over the railroad, and turn left onto an unpaved road (Oxbow Street).

At the next intersection (a T), turn left, and then continue straight ahead as you return to the village. Turn right at the paved road that follows the brook up from the village.

Then keep watch on your left for the trail up Mount Pulaski, which is a gentle climb of about 15 minutes.

After your climb, from the trailhead head back down to the green and your starting point. (From the green through the village loop, up Mount Pulaski, and return: about 3.8 miles.)

Orwell

YOU ARRIVE IN ORWELL VILLAGE by climbing or descending a hill, which makes it seem like a discovery. And it is, with its semi-oval green ringed by an unusually complete collection of 19th-century architecture.

Orwell's first settler came several years before the American Revolution, but others had ranged this wilderness for years during military campaigns centered on Fort Ticonderoga, a French and later British garrison directly across the lake in New York. The Green Mountain Boys captured the fort in 1775, and in 1776 Colonial forces built another fort on the Vermont side of the lake, named it Mount Independence, and constructed a bridge between the two. The Americans fled both Fort Ti and the Mount in July 1777, and thereafter the Vermont outpost returned to field and forest. It is now the largest undisturbed Revolutionary War site in the country and a state-owned historic site.

In the village at the corner of the leafy green stands the classical, red brick First Congregational Church, topped by a polygonal belfry with a green dome and weathervane that is visible for miles. Across the way there is a house-turned-library, with marble fireplaces and a trace of domestic coziness inside. A mini-fortress of a bank, with Gothic pointed arches of green and purple slate, was an 1878 addition to the banker's house. His successor still lives there, and money still passes to tellers through brass grilles. The general store, town hall, and school are also on the green, and it remains at the center of village life. (The eighth grade holds its graduation ceremony there, in front of the white bandstand.) As you walk elsewhere along the village's purple slate sidewalks, note the occasional hitching post or marble mounting block in front of the well-maintained 19th-century homes.

The surrounding countryside is part of the Champlain Valley, with the Green Mountains in the east and the blue-gray Adirondacks of New York State in the west. Many farmers raised Merino sheep for wool in the first half of the 19th century; later they concentrated on selling sheep, cattle, and horses for breeding stock. Today you are likely to encounter a modest flock of sheep, several riding horses, and large brick farmhouses along the back roads, evidence of an earlier prosperity.

Apple orchards thrive here in the relatively mild lakeside climate. McIntosh, Vermont's favorite variety, is related to the Fameuse, which was first grown in the Champlain Valley by the French in the 1750s. In the spring, pink blossoms cover the twisting tree branches in every orchard, and in the fall, red fruit weighs down their boughs. Between these orchards and encroaching second-growth forest, the remaining hay fields and pastures of Orwell's farms allow you intermittent glimpses of this long-tamed landscape.

In the village at the corner of the leafy green stands the classical, red brick First Congregational Church, topped by a polygonal belfry.

BEGIN YOUR WALK at the village green (on Vermont Route 73). Head east about two blocks and make a right onto Sanford Road. Go uphill past the brick Catholic church on into the countryside.

In about three-quarters of a mile, amidst orchards, take your first left onto Conkey Hill Road and walk a similar distance to the T intersection with Robinson Road, where you will make another left and begin back downhill.

At the next intersection with the paved Vermont Route 73, turn left and return to the village. (From the green back to the green, round-trip: about 3.5 miles.)

A side-trip to Mount Independence, where there are miles of hiking trails among the archeological remains of the historic fortress, is highly recommended (follow the signs from Vermont Route 73 west of the village).

Peacham

AROUND THE LEAFY CROSSROADS of Peacham, the scene seems oddly familiar. The white church and red barn side by side with mountains in the background. Have we been here before? In a way we have, for this tableau is one of the most photographed in New England. The image resonates with the interlacing of people, institutions, and even animals that are the heart of a rural village. This peaceful scene, among hills that seem to hold the world at bay, is balm for a visitor to Peacham.

Settled in 1776, Peacham is one of the highland towns that developed along the Bayley-Hazen Military Road, which opened a path through the wilderness. With no river or railroad, Peacham was always a stop on the road to somewhere else. In 1797 the town chose to be the site of the county grammar school rather than the county courthouse, and Peacham Academy remained the town school well into this century. By the mid-1800s Peacham served surrounding farms with a tannery, shoemaker and harness maker, saw and gristmills, and makers of wooden rakes and boxes. All used the raw materials of local farms and forest.

The village grew around a four corners with only a tiny grass triangle near the center, where a post bristling with timeworn signs points the way to neighboring towns. Trees arch over the roads, and well-kept white frame and red brick houses, some with barns connected, date from the late 1700s to late 1800s. Many a house might now be owned by a professor who spends the summer here, a writer, or a retired couple attracted to the village's pleasant aspect. The red clapboard general store, built in 1870, is an updated variation of the real thing. Its bulletin boards on the porch are still crammed with notices of what's happening—as in most villages, it is more than you'd expect. The simple dignity of the white 1806 Congregational church, its tall front windows looking over blossom-filled window boxes, is matched by the placid cows grazing beside it. Peacham is much as it was over a hundred years ago with nearly every structure built before 1900 and in use today.

Fields define the edge of the village. A walk on back roads takes you into a high, hilly, forested landscape with occasional stone walls. Across open farm fields are stunning views of the White Mountains rising beyond the Connecticut River Valley. In late September the leaves of maples and birches fire up among dark evergreens, and soon the roadsides are deep in drifting crimson and yellow leaves. And looking down on the village, you see that classic scene of a red barn and a tapering white church steeple.

Settled in 1776, Peacham is one of the highland towns that developed along the Bayley-Hazen Military Road, which opened a path through the wilderness. Peacham was always a stop on the road to somewhere else.

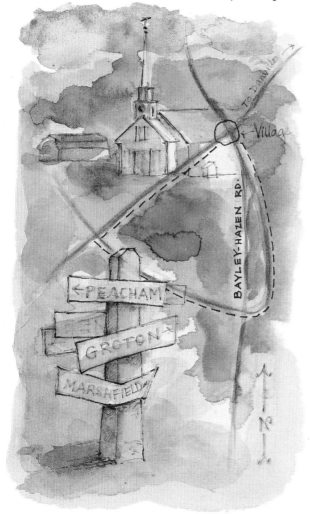

BEGIN YOUR WALK at the four corners in Peacham village. Head south on the Bayley-Hazen Road and bear left as the original military road turns to dirt.

Walk down between the rows of maples past the 18th-century Elkins Tavern on the left, follow the road through a farm as it bears right, cross the paved road, and continue on dirt for about another half mile.

Amid hay fields take your next right, go uphill past the cemetery and a commemorative green, and continue past the Congregational church to your starting point. (Round-trip: about 1.8 miles.)

To extend your walk, take a left at the cemetery onto the Cabot Road, go about a half-mile, turn right onto Ha' Penny Road.

After about three-quarters of a mile, make your next right onto Penny Street, bear right after the road crosses a brook, and make your next right onto the Bayley-Hazen Road, which will take you back to your starting point. (This route will add about 3.5 miles to your walk.)

Proctor

A VISIT TO PROCTOR is a visit to the birthplace of some familiar national monuments. The marble bridge, the high school, even the sidewalks, are made of the very same glistening white marble used to build the U.S. Supreme Court building and the Lincoln Memorial. All of it was quarried in or near the village of Proctor.

The first settlers began farming in the 1770s, but it was in 1836 that marble quarrying began here on the west side of Otter Creek. Much of Proctor village is built on marble outcrops and on piles of marble waste from quarrying operations nearby.

By 1880 Redfield Proctor consolidated a cluster of area operations into the Vermont Marble Company and began importing skilled Italian marble workers to quarry and shape the stone. By 1891 Vermont Marble was the largest marble company in the world. In 1908 at Proctor's funeral 3,000 workers and 7,000 others stood in a snowstorm to watch the casket pass. Today the successor company operates no quarries in Proctor, but there's an exhibit on the marble industry. The flavor of a tidy, front-porch kind of company town remains.

Around the green on Main Street are echoes of the industrial past—the marble factory whose yard is stacked with blocks and slabs of white stone, the company's hillside headquarters constructed of marble blocks, a square stone and clapboard recreation hall built for workers, and the quarters of the former company cooperative store, now home to the post office and supermarket. A short riverside path behind the library leads to a bird's-eye view of the marble works sited at a set of falls on Otter Creek, which was and is its power source.

Elsewhere in the village, Ormsbee Avenue on a hill east of Vermont Route 3 is lined with imposing colonial-style houses built in the early 20th century for company managers. The grandest is Redfield Proctor Jr.'s, a brick house with marble touches on a sweeping lawn behind a low stone wall. On Meadow Street north of the marble works, rows of identical slate-roofed duplexes with matching porches show how many workers lived in Proctor in the 1890s.

Just past the last house in the village in any direction begins an undulating landscape that borders Otter Creek, with rolling meadows and fields. Walking the Gorham Bridge Road, you follow roughly the route of the pre-Revolutionary Crown Point Military Road. It is still bounded by trees, and for a while the meandering Otter Creek bends close by. At a narrow point watched over by curious Holsteins is the 1841 Gorham covered bridge. Walking through the dim interior, you can see the sturdy exposed lattice truss of the bridge. Builders covered bridges to protect them from the elements, so the structures would last. More than a century and a half later, it appears they did it right.

The first settlers began farming in the 1770s, but it was in 1836 that marble quarrying began here on the west side of Otter Creek. Much of Proctor village is built on hills of marble.

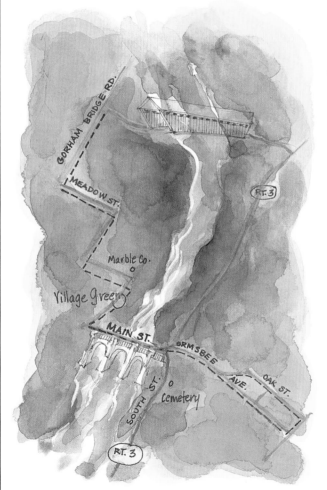

BEGIN YOUR WALK at the village green, head east across the Marble Bridge, cross Vermont Route 3, and walk up Ormsbee Avenue.

Continue past Governor Redfield Proctor Jr.'s red brick house to Warner Avenue, turn left and then left again onto Oak Street, where you will loop back to Ormsbee and down again across Route 3 to the green.

Then head up Main Street past the marble works and make your first right onto North Street, where you will pass through a neighborhood of late-19th-century workers' housing before arriving at the T intersection with Meadow Street.

Turn left and then right onto Gorham Bridge Road, walk out the covered bridge, and return to the village and the green by the same route. (From the green, through the Ormsbee Avenue loop back to the green, and out Gorham Bridge and back is about 4.7 miles.)

Shoreham

O N A TRANQUIL SUMMER MORNING, it is easy to imagine the village of Shoreham much as it was a century ago. Except for a rare passing car, there is no hum of modern life. Bird song is the only sound.

The town was settled in 1766 by veterans of the French and Indian War. Many had previously traveled through on the Crown Point Military Road, which ran from the Connecticut River across the dense forest that was to become Vermont to the French, and then British, fort at Crown Point across Lake Champlain. In the early 19th century, Shoreham became a prosperous sheep-raising center. It had 41,188 sheep in 1840, the largest number of any town in the state. Today its fertile, flat Champlain Valley fields have turned to dairy farming and apple growing.

The two streets of the village meet at the green, which, befitting a rural town, resembles a wide field. There a white clapboard inn has provided lodging since 1828 and a row of 19th-century houses stand with fanlights over their doors or decorative wooden flourishes. From a small rise the commanding red brick Congregational church (1846), designed by local master builder James Lamb, overlooks the green. In the "waste not, want not" tradition, residents have found new uses for both the 1885 Universalist church, with its corner bell tower and large stained glass window, and the 1811 Shoreham Academy next door. A new school behind the old is the only new construction on the green since the town library was built in 1908.

Beyond the village the countryside opens with a view of the broad valley farmland, once the floor of a vast glacial lake and later a saltwater sea that reached the foothills of the mountains seen in the distance. Farms are larger here than in many places in Vermont, spread out on the less rocky, fairly level terrain. Walking the unmarked dirt roads, you feel an openness and expansiveness rarely sensed in a state elsewhere hedged by hills. This is Vermont's big-sky country. With the Green Mountains in the east and the Adirondacks across the lake in the west, this peaceful yet quietly busy farming community of apple orchards and Holsteins is framed by good views of two ranges.

Walking the unmarked dirt roads, you feel an openness and expansiveness rarely sensed in a state elsewhere hedged by hills. This is Vermont's big-sky country.

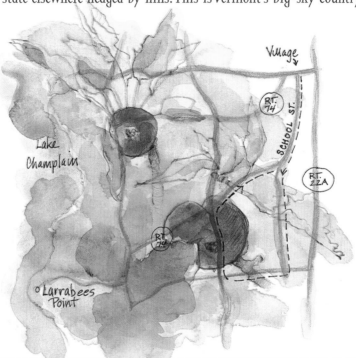

Village

RT. 74

SCHOOL ST.

Lake Champlain

RT. 22A

RT. 74

o Larrabees Point

BEGIN YOUR WALK heading down the west side of the village green (on School Street) past the churches and school. Continue south along the road into the countryside as the road turns to dirt and walk for over 2 miles, passing a first right and then making the second right, where you will be heading west.

Proceed less than a mile to a four corners, turn right, go about a mile, and at the intersection with a paved road (Vermont Route 74), take a right onto the dirt road heading northeast.

In over a mile, this will bring you back to School Street, where you can turn left and return to

the village. (From the green, around the loop, and back to the green is about 6.5 miles.)

(A side-trip out Vermont Route 74 to Larrabee's Point takes you near where Ethan Allen and his Green Mountain Boys crossed the lake in 1775 to capture Fort Ticonderoga from the

British in a surprise night raid. The store there at the point was built of limestone probably brought over in 1823 from the crumbling walls of the fort. A tiny ferry still plies the narrow lake here on a water route dating from before the Revolution.)

Strafford

*T*HERE IS STILL A LINK BETWEEN farming and Strafford, a well-preserved early-19th-century agricultural village, although now the farms are likely to be horse rather than dairy farms, their pastures trimmed with white board fences. The tidy village harmoniously circles a sloping green on which towers a commanding white meeting house with a two-tiered steeple and spire. Much of the surrounding countryside is enveloped by forest.

Strafford was settled in 1768 by people from Connecticut who located just north of the present village and organized the first Baptist church in the state. The community later drifted south when the Meeting House was built in 1799 along the route from Montpelier to Boston. Strafford is a good example of a rural village center, where commerce and social institutions located to serve many surrounding small farms. It is the kind of place that is threatened elsewhere in Vermont, where housing and commercial development blur the distinction between village and countryside. Recognizing and valuing a compact village like Strafford is the first step toward maintaining it.

Strafford village spreads around the green and extends slightly to the south. Its unified appearance is achieved through the similar scale, spacing, and orientation to the road of the houses and commercial buildings, as well as the predominant use of wood as a building material. There are no modern intrusions;

all 30 of the village buildings were constructed before the middle of the 19th century.

This is not to say that all of the buildings are the same. At one end of the village stands the outstanding but simple meeting house with its central clock tower and steeple. At the south end is the captivating salmon-colored Justin Morrill Homestead, dripping with wooden, scroll-sawn trim and castlelike details. This 17-room Gothic fantasy and its outbuildings were designed and built in 1848-1853 by Morrill, a blacksmith's son who represented Vermont in Congress for 44 years and authored the landmark Land Grant Colleges Act. With period interiors and many family furnishings intact, it is now owned by the state (open mid-May to mid-Oct., Wed.-Sun. 9:30-5:30).

Strafford village lies along the west branch of the Ompompanoosuc River in a valley between two ridges whose thickly wooded slopes lend it a green backdrop. In the 20th century, as the surrounding small hill farms became less profitable, old farmhouses were acquired as second homes or by people interested in riding. Many of the high meadows now pasture horses, sometimes Morgans, Vermont's own breed, which originated in nearby Randolph Center in 1795. But most of the hillsides here are woods, where miles of stonewall remind you of the early farms that made the beautiful village that remains below.

The tidy village harmoniously circles a sloping green. There are no modern intrusions; all 30 of the village buildings were constructed before the middle of the 19th century.

BEGIN YOUR WALK at the green and explore the village. Then head to the right of the Meeting House up the River Road nearly three-quarters of a mile and take a right on Old City Road.

Go uphill as the road follows one side of Old City Brook, and when the road levels out and the forest opens up, make the next left, which will take you across the brook.

Immediately on your left there is a drive to a picnic area overlooking Old City Falls, a source of waterpower for the earliest settlers.

Return to the village by the same route. (From the green to Old City Falls and return: about 3 miles.)

Waitsfield

WAITSFIELD WAS A FARMING VILLAGE before three ski areas overtook it. It lies in the valley of the Mad River with the Green Mountains looming beside it. Although there is new development, it is often at the base of the ski slopes on the mountains and hardly noticeable in the village below, with its row of minimally refurbished, old-fashioned commercial buildings and even a covered bridge.

Since the early 1960s, absorbing the growth of ski-related development without disturbing traditional village settlement patterns and altering the rural nature of the valley has been the planning challenge.

Waitsfield was settled in 1789 by a colonel in Washington's army. Lawmakers decided against making the centrally located town the capital of the new state of Vermont; residents instead developed its natural gifts from the river, its fertile valley, and the dense mountain forests. Farms in the valley have remained an important part of the town through the present. (The whole Mad River Valley north of the village has recently been listed in the National Register of Historic Places as a rural historic district.) Lumbering was also an important industry for Waitsfield and neighboring Warren.

Most houses along Waitsfield's main street are from the 19th century, some brick with simple lines and others frame construction with decorative flourishes. The Mad River flows swiftly behind them. The big, square, former high school (1847) is now office space; an 1894 clapboard church with an off-center belfry is an art studio; and a former carriage house is now a service station. Many of the commercial buildings have two-story porches. Two stone columns at the library's entrance lend the building an unaccustomed note of grandeur.

Leaving the village through the covered bridge (1833, but restored), you have a close-up view of the river before the road begins to climb gently. From the Common Road there is a stunning view of the great ridge of Green Mountains rising west of the village. The link to the area's agricultural past is kept in some measure not only by a few remaining dairy farms but by horse farms, nurseries, and many century-old farmhouses converted to inns. One of the most unusual inns, with a round barn, is on the Warren Road. Round barns were built in Vermont in the early 1900s on the theory that they were more efficient, and a few remain.

Although the Mad River Valley is one of the state's largest ski resort areas, no billboards line the roads leading to it. Since 1967 Vermont has been the only state to ban such roadside signs. With the support of the tourist industry, which saw the advantage in an uncluttered landscape, billboards were replaced by a system of small, uniform directional signs and Travel Information Plazas. It makes a clearer lens through which to see both Vermont's past and present.

Residents developed its natural gifts from the river, its fertile valley, and the dense mountain forests. Farms in the valley have remained an important part of the town.

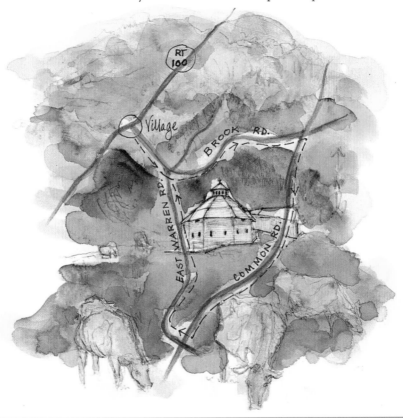

BEGIN YOUR WALK at the covered bridge in the village after exploring the main street (Vermont Route 100). Cross the bridge, head uphill, and bear left at the Y intersection.

Continue a short ways and make your first right onto the unpaved Brook Road. Follow it over a mile uphill to its T intersection with the Common Road and turn right.

While taking in the views, stroll over another mile to paved East Warren Road, make a right, and walk downhill past the Joslin Round Barn back to the first Y intersection, where you bear left to cross the covered bridge back into the village. (From the covered bridge through the loop back to the bridge: 5.9 miles.)

Woodstock

*A*N EARLY 19TH-CENTURY Woodstock resident, U.S. Senator Jacob Collamer, once remarked, "The good people of Woodstock have less incentive than others to yearn for heaven," and we can still see why. Through residents' care and with the help of local wealth, Woodstock radiates a grace and civility that rise above the onslaught of traffic and tourism that has overtaken it. Around the oval green the buildings bespeak quality: white columns, bricks mellow with time, a courthouse topped by a copper-capped cupola, and a dignified redstone library with triple round arches.

The town was granted in 1772 via a royal charter, which can be seen in the Dana House (1807), now the home of the Woodstock Historical Society. By 1791, when Vermont became the fourteenth state, the village had developed around a dam and sawmills and gristmills on the Ottauquechee River and was prominent enough to be selected as the shire town for the county. This attracted two centuries of lawyers, merchants, professionals, and others with an eye for opportunity and eventually a yen to ski. On Vermont Route 12 north of the village is a roadside marker at the site of the nation's first ski tow, a 1934 rope device powered by a Model T engine, which for a brief season made farmer Gilbert's hill pasture the biggest ski resort in the country.

An air of prosperity clings to the village with its demi-mansions, substantial 19th-century public buildings, and the mammoth Woodstock Inn on a corner near the green. The hillside Marsh-Billings-Rockefeller House was the boyhood home of George Perkins Marsh, the father of modern ecology, and later of Frederick Billings, a local boy whose fortune as a land-claims lawyer in the California gold rush added considerable space and architectural flourishes to the property in the late 1800s. It is now the summer home of Billings's granddaughter and her husband, Mary and Laurance Rockefeller, who converted the Billings model dairy farm into the Billings Farm and Museum, dedicated to illustrating what farm life in this area was like in 1890.

Like much of upland Vermont during the 19th century, the foothills of the Green Mountains that surround Woodstock were destroyed for productive farming and forestry by poor land use practices and clearcutting. Observing this profligacy, George Perkins Marsh formed his philosophy of the interconnectedness of people and their environment, and his 1864 book *Man and Nature* has a special place on the bookshelf of the ecology movement. Woodstock today is more a center for riding horses than for dairy cows, and for hobby farms rather than working ones. Both, however, keep fields open and create the patchwork landscape of fields and woods that can be viewed from the many hills surrounding the village.

An air of prosperity clings to the village with its demi-mansions, substantial 19th-century public buildings, and the mammoth Woodstock Inn on a corner near the green.

BEGIN YOUR WALK at the green and explore the village. On the river side of the green, cross over the covered bridge and go straight past River Street to Mountain Avenue.

Turn left and proceed to the small park on the right, where you can take the 2-mile path up to the top of Mount Tom, with its views up and down the river valley.

To return to the green, continue along Mountain Avenue, turn left back to River Street, and then cross the historic bridge with globe-light lampposts.

This becomes Church Street. Keep to the left and you will return to your starting point. (Not counting the hike up Mount Tom, this walk is a little under a mile.)

Bellows Falls

DOWNTOWN BELLOWS FALLS has variety. Take the Miss Bellows Falls Diner, such a fine example of a railroad-car-type diner that it is listed in the National Register of Historic Places. Then there is the tall, square clock tower of the town hall, straight out of an Italian hill town. It overlooks a village square and one of the first canals built in the United States. All of this makes for an interesting stroll through a downtown with an early 20th-century flavor.

The village is sited at a rocky 52-foot waterfall that tumbles through a gorge in the Connecticut River. Early settlers fished for migrating salmon and shad here and in 1785 built the first bridge across the Connecticut, just above the falls. As commercial river traffic increased, the canal was constructed in 1802. Bellows Falls became a flourishing travel link. The arrival of the railroad in 1848 increased the village's importance, although river traffic declined. As factories and businesses prospered, Bellows Falls entered its golden age in the early 20th century, and during those years the village acquired its present urban character, with hotels, impressive commercial blocks, and tree-lined residential streets.

After a period of economic decline that began in the 1930s, Bellows Falls in the 1970s followed a plan to improve its downtown and restore its handsome buildings. On the L-shaped square the dominant feature is the red brick town hall (1926), with its two-stage crenelated clock tower. Near the square, promi-

nent buildings from the turn of the century include the brick Centennial Block, with its elaborate decorative roofline, and the wood frame Brown Block, set off by a copper-sheathed polygonal corner tower. The former Hotel Rockingham (1883) has a harmonious ground-floor gallery of identical round-top arched doors and windows and has been restored.

What is left of Bellows Falls' rich rail, industrial, and canal history can be seen on "the Island," where big brick industrial buildings await new uses. The gorge is visible from the bridge to New Hampshire. The dam and hydroelectric powerhouse with a visitors' gallery are just off the square, as is the Adams Grist Mill and Museum, dating from 1831.

The domestic side of Bellows Falls' history comes into view in the neighborhoods west of downtown (what one local group calls "the front porch capital of the world"), where turn-of-the-century houses sport decorative elements ranging from towers to fish-scale slate shingles. A short detour onto Church Street is worthwhile for the stone Emmanuel Episcopal Church, designed by noted architect Richard Upjohn, best known for Trinity Church in New York's Wall Street district. Further west, streets quickly go uphill. With almost no land for agriculture, residents historically have looked to transportation, commerce, and industry for their livelihoods, as they still do today.

*Early settlers fished for migrating salmon and shad here
and in 1785 built the first bridge across the Connecticut, just above the falls.*

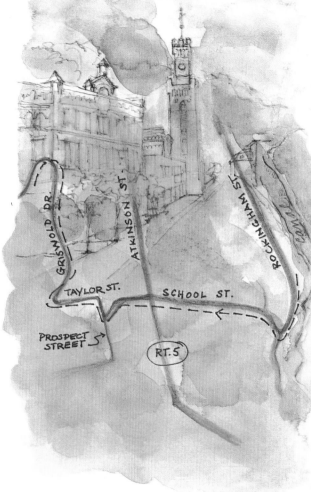

BEGIN YOUR WALK downtown on Rockingham Street on the square. Explore downtown, Canal Street, and the Island.

Then head south on Rockingham Street from the square, and after you pass a retaining wall on your right, make a right turn (of almost 180 degrees) onto Church Street.

Walk the short distance past a memorial green, make a detour to see the Episcopal church if you wish, but turn left onto School Street and head west through the residential neighborhood.

Cross the busy Atkinson Street (U.S. Route 5) to School Street Extension and continue as it curves south, then take a sharp right onto Prospect Street and a left onto Taylor Street.

Head up to its intersection with Griswold Drive, make a right, and head uphill. You can turn back when you encounter new housing about a half mile up the hill.

Return by the same route or pick another through the neighborhood to see some different houses. It shouldn't be too hard to find your way back to downtown, but if you need to, ask someone! (From downtown to one-half mile up Griswold and return: about 2 miles.)

Bennington

*H*ISTORY GRACES OLD BENNINGTON (the original settlement on the hill) with an air of nobility. The center of the first town chartered in the territory that became Vermont, it was no transient village on the way to somewhere else. It soon became a substantial group of handsome houses. Nowhere else are the designs for picket fences so varied and elegant: white slats dip like garlands or step their way down the hill in stages, their posts crowned with wooden urns or balls. The Catamount Tavern, where the Green Mountain Boys met and plotted, is long gone. But on its site a bronze catamount atop a polished granite base silently surveys the anachronistic stream of traffic roaring through this village to the newer Bennington down the hill.

Bennington was first settled by a Massachusetts soldier who camped on the hillside here as he returned home from service in the French and Indian War. A few years later, in 1761, he returned with a group of families who founded the town. On the hilltop the Bennington Battle Monument, a 306-foot granite shaft said to be the tallest battle monument in the world, towers over the village. It marks the Revolutionary War Battle of Bennington in 1777, when a collection of New England militiamen routed the British, who were attempting to capture supplies stored on this spot. August 16, Bennington Battle Day, is a state holiday in Vermont.

At the heart of the village is the Old First Church, erected in 1806 by Vermont's first organized church, founded in 1762. This building by Lavius Fillmore, considered one of the most beautiful in the state, has a simple white clapboard facade, graceful three-part Palladian window, and graduated bell tower. Beside it is the Old Burying Ground, where the haunting wide eyes of round-faced angel carvings peer down the ages from time-streaked stones. Three centuries lie here, including dead from both sides in the Battle of Bennington, town founders, and poet Robert Frost, who chose the epitaph "He had a lover's quarrel with the world."

Across the narrow green that divides Monument Avenue is the oldest inn in Vermont, the slightly sagging, long unpainted Walloomsac Inn, which operated from 1775 until recent years. Up the avenue from the church and inn, marble sidewalks climb the gentle grade past large, mostly 19th-century, white frame houses and the Old Academy (1821), built of orange-toned, handmade bricks arranged in a long-short pattern.

This village overlooks the Walloomsac River Valley, where hills rise to the north and the forested flanks of the Green Mountains dominate the east. The Village of Bennington, with its historic downtown and industry, clusters in the valley below. To the west are scattered patches of woods and some summer houses from the early years of the 20th century. Farther west, as the land becomes more level, farms and orchards still define this landscape that people have long since tamed for their homes and livelihood.

Bennington was first settled by a Massachusetts soldier who camped
on the hillside here as he returned home from service in the French and Indian War.
A few years later he returned with a group of families who founded the town.

BEGIN YOUR WALK at the Old First Church and Burying Ground. (The graveyard is always open, and if you are lucky the church may be, too.)

Cross the street to the Walloomsac Inn, proceed west on Vermont Route 9 about 1.5 miles to Gypsy Lane, and turn right.

Go about half a mile, turn right onto Walloomsac Road, and proceed east to the Bennington Battle Monument (it's worth a ride to the top, if it's open).

Then head south down Monument Avenue, past the Old Academy and Catamount Tavern site to where you started. (Round-trip: approximately 4 miles.)

Brattleboro

*I*T IS SAID THAT BRATTLEBORO is a college town without a college—a good description of a likely first impression. The lively downtown streets look much as they did 100 years ago but now offer the quirky discoveries in which good college towns specialize. Buildings have converted from church to shop, from railroad station to art museum, from house to office, as new life continues in old shells.

Brattleboro was chartered in 1753 to William Brattle Jr. and his associates of Boston and was settled in the 1760s on what is now Main Street. The Estey Organ Company, established in 1866, developed into the village's most important industry as it fed a national craving for parlor organs to become the largest organ manufacturer in the country. (Its remarkable slate-sided buildings still stand on Birge Street.) Ravaged by flood and fire in 1869, Brattleboro began rebuilding in a more lavish style. Although the village remained the dominant commercial and cultural center in southeast Vermont through the first half of the 20th century, many credit a quiet invasion of the counterculture in the 1960s and 1970s with reinvigorating Brattleboro and giving it much of its current style.

The historic center of Brattleboro covers the five-block Main Street. At its north end is the Wells Fountain (1890), designed by a native son, noted architect William Rutherford Mead. It features classical columns and stands on the spot where his brother, sculptor Larkin Mead, on a freezing New Year's Eve in 1856 created a snow angel to delight the town. A marble replica of the angel is in the Brooks Memorial Library nearby. On a knoll opposite the fountain, municipal offices occupy the marble-trimmed, 1884 brick high school. The tall, white graduated clock tower and spire of the wood frame Congregational church (1842) rise over this section of the street, which until the 1930s had large residences as well as public buildings.

The next three commercial blocks are anchored by the four-story brick Brooks House (1872), which wraps around a corner, its central tower overlooking the busy intersection. (It is now apartments.) Across the street an ornate iron pedestal street clock marks time on gilt roman numerals. At Main Street and Flat Street, the Latchis Hotel (1936) stands out as the only example of the Art Deco style. Beautifully restored inside and out, it includes not only a hotel but a theater and restaurant. Over a little iron bridge over the Whetstone Brook is the one-story stone Union Station, nicely adapted for use as the Brattleboro Museum and Art Center, with a full calendar of events from May 15 to November 1.

The hills on either side of the river are rocky and wooded. Looking down from their summits, you find that Brattleboro seems far below, at rest along the great sweep of the river amid the hilly contours of the land rising from the valley.

The lively downtown streets look much as they did 100 years ago but now offer the quirky discoveries in which good college towns specialize.

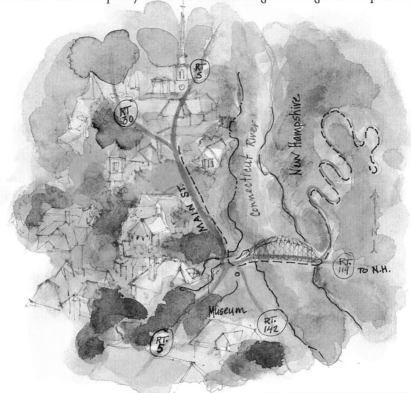

BEGIN YOUR WALK on upper Main Street (the junction of Vermont Route 30 and U.S. Route 5) near the Wells Fountain.

Head down through downtown, cross Whetstone Brook, turn left onto Bridge Street, pass the Brattleboro Museum and Art Center, and cross the historic steel truss bridge into New Hampshire (New Hampshire Route 119).

Once you have crossed the river, turn onto a short road on the left, which leads to a trail system on Wantastiquet Mountain. To reach several lookouts over Brattleboro, avoid side trails; the main trail leads to the top of the mountain.

(From the Wells Fountain to the trailhead in New Hampshire is a little over one-half mile. The trail to the top of the mountain is 2 miles, one-way. From the fountain to the mountaintop and back is about 5 miles.)

Chester

HERE ARE REALLY THREE CHESTERS. The main village has a long, narrow green with the old academy and cemetery lying peacefully on one side and shops and an inn full of activity on the other. North Chester, a mile to the north, is also known as the "Stone Village" because of its two rows of stone houses bordering the highway. And in between, Chester Depot grew around the railroad station, which once carried away soapstone from nearby quarries.

The three Chesters evolved because two religious denominations couldn't agree on a central location to build a union church. In 1780 the town voted to divide into southern and northern sections, south for the Baptists and north for the Congregationalists. Rival villages grew up along the two main roads in town (now Vermont Routes 11 and 103), but by 1830 things had tipped in favor of the south village, which had the post office and finally a new union church. The south village became a thriving commercial center, and the north village gradually became residential. Chester Depot was a sufficiently neutral site to build the town hall. (Previously, town meetings alternated between the other two villages.)

Chester is very nearly as it was in the late 1800s, a collection of buildings in that century's many popular architectural styles. Most changes have been in the uses of buildings rather than changes in the buildings themselves. Instead of tearing down and building anew, Chester adapted, allowing it to continue to live and work in its own three-dimensional history. It is easy to imagine the village green as it looked long ago, since the commercial activity now lining its south side is in former residences. The plainer ones are from the first half of the 19th century, and the more exuberant ones, with asymmetrical towers, are from the latter half. Anchoring this row of houses is a large three-story inn, whose long porch at the edge of the street seems almost like the town's front porch. Across the green the red brick, early-19th-century academy, now the historical society, has the impressive bulk and dignity that say "school" no matter what the structure's use today.

A mile away up Church Street is the "Stone Village," a row of houses, a church, and a school all constructed in the 1830s and 1840s of locally quarried gneiss and mica schist. This gray stone is found nearby cropping up in almost vertical layers 4 to 6 inches thick. It is used to build walls in a style called Snecked Ashlar, where the irregular slabs are arranged on edge in random patterns, almost like a mosaic.

The villages of Chester are in the valley of the Williams River, which cuts through hilly terrain as many streams feed it on its way down to the Connecticut River. Farming has declined, and the countryside is now mainly forested, a popular place for second-home owners. As in other such spots, many of them eventually become residents, ensuring new keepers for old houses and the land.

The three Chesters — the main village, the "Stone Village," and Chester Depot —
evolved because two religious denominations couldn't agree on a
central location to build a union church.

BEGIN YOUR WALK at the Chester Village green on Vermont Route 11.

Proceed east to the junction with Vermont Route 103, and head north past the railroad station through Chester Depot and across the Williams River to the Stone Village.

Just past the North Chester Cemetery, make a left onto Church Street, which crosses the river again and takes you back to Chester Village, where a left will return you to the green. (Round-trip: about 2.75 miles.)

You may wish to detour down the road heading south from the green, which crosses the Middle Branch of the Williams River on a suspension bridge. About a half mile farther west on Vermont Route 11, a dirt road, Lovers Lane, heads north into a densely wooded area of former farms, now overgrown.

Dorset

CLUSTERED AROUND its long, slim green, Dorset village is gilded by prosperity, smoothing out any wrinkle in the unified scene. Everything is painted a crisp white and well tended. Forest green or black shutters bracket each window. The general store next to the post office sports a smart awning over a marble step. The inn on the green is the picture of simple dignity behind a line of pillars. Quiet busyness marks the scene as residents do their errands here in the village center as they have for 200 years. Only the type of resident has changed, as many houses are now second homes, their owners living here part-time.

In 1776, when this area was part of the New Hampshire Grants (Vermont land being parceled out by both New York and New Hampshire at that time), a meeting was held in West Dorset where delegates signed a declaration of rights proclaiming the independence of Vermont. By 1785, residents had opened the first marble quarry in America. Located south of the village, the quarry eventually provided marble for such buildings as the New York Public Library. But the high-quality marble ran out, and the quarry closed in 1921, becoming a popular swimming hole. Since the early 20th century, Dorset has attracted artists, writers, and actors; the Dorset Playhouse still presents a full summer season.

The village developed in the valley of the West Branch River, spreading around the green and along the river road. Between 1800 and 1850, marble money built many of the white frame residences on the green, which itself has a marble slab sidewalk. These substantial houses have been treated with respect over the years, most retaining their original appearance, including marble steps. The Dorset Inn, with a tall square-pillared porch, has operated continually since 1796. Just past the green stands the solid gray marble Congregational church (1911).

In the countryside along West Road stands a remarkable marble house, the first two-story residence of locally quarried marble built in Vermont and probably the nation. Made in 1802 of sand-colored, slightly irregular marble blocks, with a 1922 marble addition to the rear, it faces the wooded hills of the Taconic Range, which surrounds Dorset and extends south into Massachusetts and west into New York. East of the village, Lower Hollow Road follows the upper reaches of the Mettawee River, while Upper Hollow Road climbs for mountain views across the few farm fields and areas kept open by residents of the scattered houses along the road. In Dorset as in other Vermont towns where few farms remain, part-time or nonfarming residents are often the caretakers of what land is kept open, thereby maintaining the state's appealing patchwork landscape.

Since the early 20th century, Dorset has attracted artists, writers, and actors; the Dorset Playhouse still presents a full summer season.

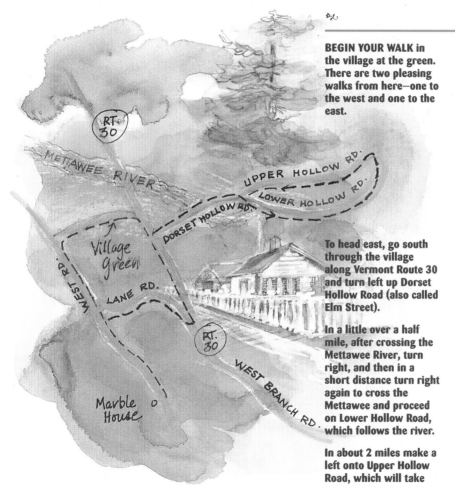

BEGIN YOUR WALK in the village at the green. There are two pleasing walks from here—one to the west and one to the east.

To head east, go south through the village along Vermont Route 30 and turn left up Dorset Hollow Road (also called Elm Street).

In a little over a half mile, after crossing the Mettawee River, turn right, and then in a short distance turn right again to cross the Mettawee and proceed on Lower Hollow Road, which follows the river.

In about 2 miles make a left onto Upper Hollow Road, which will take you back in about 2 miles to where you first crossed the river; from there return to the green by the same route. (From the green through the Hollow Road loop and return to the green: 6.3 miles.)

To see the West Dorset area, follow the road along the green heading southwest, cross the West Branch, and at the next intersection turn left onto West Road.

Go over a mile through the next intersections left and right, and on your right you will see the 1802 marble house.

Retrace your steps to the road heading east (on your right), and proceed on that road across the West Branch to the paved Vermont Route 30.

Turn left and return to the village and the green. (From the green to the marble house and return to the green: 4.8 miles.)

Grafton

HE VILLAGE OF GRAFTON has the good fortune not only to be restored to picture-book quality but to be situated on roads that heighten a visitor's sense of anticipation. Through thick woods the road from the north descends a steep hill, and those from the south and east round a sharp curve. The village takes you by surprise in more ways than one.

Grafton's peak of prosperity came in the decades before the Civil War, when it was humming with industry. Mills wove cloth out of wool from the town's 10,000 sheep, and thirteen quarries produced soapstone that was converted into useful items such as footwarmers, sinks, and inkwells. Soapstone, which conducts heat and is still used in griddles and wood stoves, is so soft it can be cut by a saw nearly as easily as a pine board. Grafton men fought in the Civil War, and as in many Vermont towns, many never returned. Daisy Turner, the daughter of an ex-slave and Civil War veteran who moved to Grafton, lived most of her 104 years on a farm here. She became a remarkable source of oral history, recalling with exceptional clarity her life and accounts of the war told by her father (she appeared in the PBS series "The Civil War").

To stroll through Grafton is to see the architectural styles favored from around 1815 to 1850. There are decorative but restrained treatments in glass around doors and windows, columns and other classical elements from that period, and the use of brick as well

as wood. Grafton looks so perfectly kept because, since the early 1960s when a benefactor formed the Windham Foundation to restore the declining village, nothing has been left to chance. All wires went underground and the Old Tavern, a brick roadside inn from 1801, was restored. The centerpiece of the village, the inn has generous double porches with rocking chairs and a clapboard third story added in the 1860s. Its facade was kept but the inside updated. Note the old stone doorstep inscription: "Montani Semper Liberi" (mountaineers are always free).

Other notable buildings are the little white firehouse, which began as a school in 1830; well-tended residences owned by people attracted to living in such a picture-book village; and two churches—a white wood frame one and a brick one. The brick church dates from the 1830s and is the visual terminus of the west end of the village. Its anomalous white clapboard rear wall was added in 1883, when the bricks were taken from that wall to lengthen the church.

The countryside that surrounds Grafton is every bit as harmonious as the village itself. A state forest accounts for many acres of woods, scattered through with enormous boulders that the earth's upheavals tossed this way. The Saxtons River and its branches meet at the village, so water and bridges are integral to the town. Farming is no longer a part of Grafton, although the Windham Foundation maintains a flock of sheep on the hills north of town.

To stroll through Grafton is to see the architectural styles favored
from around 1815 to 1850. The village takes you by surprise in more ways than one.

BEGIN YOUR WALK at
the brick church at the
west end of Main Street.
Veer right onto Middle-
town Road and walk

through woods lined
with stone walls for
about 2 miles (ignore
two short roads first on
the right and then the

left) until its intersection
with Vermont Route 121
(unpaved). Turn right
and follow the rocky
Saxtons River back to

the white church in the
village. (From the brick
church out and back to
the white church: 4.1
miles.)

Landgrove

*T*HERE IS A BRIGADOON QUALITY to Landgrove, where all paved roads cease as they enter the town. It adds to the feeling that time is unwinding on the densely wooded roads in one of the smallest towns in Vermont. There is no store or post office in the village, just a tiny cluster of buildings on a curve in the road.

The town is hatchet shaped—2 miles long and at some points only half a mile wide. This odd shape is explained by errors that happen when mapping a mountainous area—the leftover often called a gore. When Bennington County was laid out, a piece of land which hadn't been included because of the mountainous topography became Landgrove, a smaller-than-usual town whose boundaries were finally established in 1833.

At one time Landgrove had a post office, mill, church, coach inn, general store, and cheese factory. The principal village was called Clarksville, but after the post office closed, maps show it as North Landgrove. By the late 1920s about the only things left were the church, farmhouses whose land was gradually being reclaimed by shrubs and woods, and the deteriorating village houses. At that time a new resident restored his own house and during the Depression began buying others to restore and sell to people who were looking for life off the beaten track, full-time or seasonally.

A village walk and a country walk are really the same thing in Landgrove, since the only indication of the village is that a few buildings are closer together. The Landgrove houses here and along the woodsy unpaved roads are often frame Cape-style homes of one or one-and-a-half stories. In the village the original store and post office is now a residence, and the Community Church is small and white with double front doors. The town hall leaves clues it was once a school: a belfry and the four big windows on two sides that were prescribed by state law in 1904 to flood the interior with natural light.

All of Landgrove seems far away from modern life, let alone the ski areas that are actually only a few miles away. It lies in a basin of the Green Mountains, including part of the Green Mountain National Forest, at about 1,800 feet. Some miles to the west the mountains average over 3,000 feet. Occasional views through the woods are of peaks white or green (depending on the season), several with ski trails cut through the trees. A few small farms that raise vegetables or sheep are all that remain of the many hill farms that once supported families here. Distinctive homes are now much more common than barns (which are also likely to have been made into distinctive homes!).

Just a tiny cluster of buildings on a curve in the road, all of Landgrove seems far away from modern life, let alone the ski areas that are actually only a few miles away.

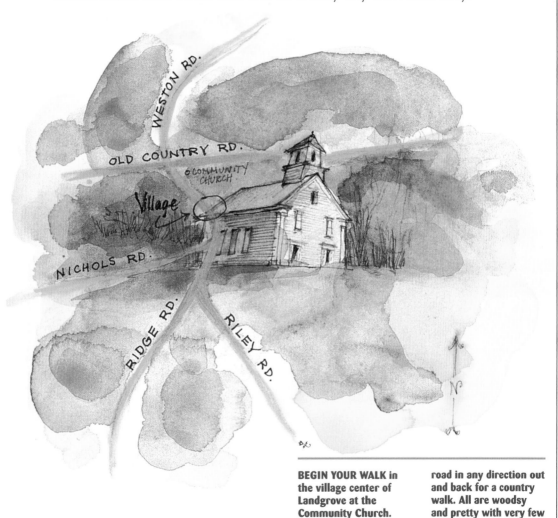

BEGIN YOUR WALK in the village center of Landgrove at the Community Church. From there take any road in any direction out and back for a country walk. All are woodsy and pretty with very few houses.

Manchester Village

MANCHESTER HAS NEVER BEEN an ordinary Vermont village. Hospitality is its business and has been since before the Revolution. Here, the streets are a little wider, the lawns a little deeper, the sidewalks white marble. Mature trees shade the broad main street in long rows, and along one side of the street is a veritable white wall of an old summer hotel, the Equinox, with colonnades marching along its great length. The 19th-century hotel, now a year-round resort, has long hosted presidents and the wealthy, their thirst for scenery satisfied by the grand setting of Manchester—at rest on a foothill of Mount Equinox in the Taconic Range overlooking the valley of the Batten Kill and the Green Mountains to the east.

In the early 19th century, Manchester developed not only as a mecca for travelers but also a center of town and county life. Among the taverns and inns, residents built handsome public buildings, such as the brick county courthouse and the gray stone Burr and Burton Seminary. At mid-century much commercial life migrated down the hill to Manchester Center to greet the arrival of the railroad. In the late 19th and early 20th centuries many folks built summer houses for leisurely stays until winter closed in. Among them was Robert Todd Lincoln, who in 1905 built Hildene, the estate where his descendants lived until 1975, and which is now open to the public.

Today as you ascend the hill from the Center, much of the hustle and tangle of traffic falls away as you approach the serenity of Manchester village. Laid out along the road, the village seems a harmonious whole, with its white church, courthouse, inns, and residences along the wide central street. Fences were forbidden; deep lawns blend into one generous greensward. Houses generally have marble foundations and are usually white with large front porches to catch the summer breeze. The Equinox Hotel looks like two three-tiered wedding cakes; its first section opened in 1853 and was later connected to a neighboring hotel. The whole thing now rambles much as connected farmhouses and barns do in Vermont.

The view over the valley from Union Street is of well-tamed countryside, backed by the wooded slopes of the Green Mountains. Two manicured green velvet golf courses flank the road that descends to the Batten Kill, a famous trout stream. Some farms remain in the narrow river valley, but the feeling of the countryside is generally of tended grounds, clumps of trees spared for effect, and stone walls helping keep nature tidy. The forest on Mount Equinox, however, touches the edge of the village at Prospect Street. Overall, it is an attractive scene, its natural beauty enhanced by the works of humanity.

The view over the valley from Union Street is of well-tamed countryside,
backed by the wooded slopes of the Green Mountains.
Two golf courses flank the road that descends to the Batten Kill.

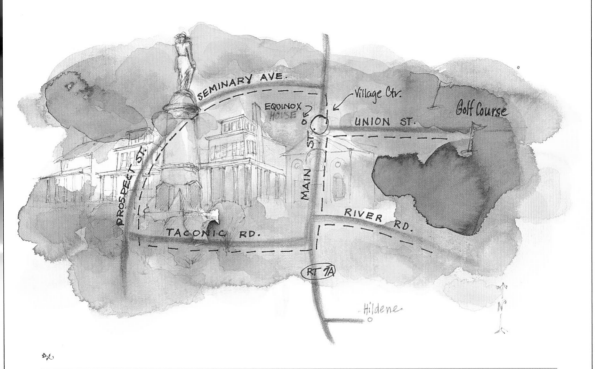

BEGIN YOUR WALK in front of the Equinox on Main Street (Vermont Route 7A). Head north and make the first left onto Seminary Avenue, which leads to the 1831 Burr and Burton Seminary.

Continue to the left along Prospect Street to its intersection with Taconic Road, make a left, and walk almost a half-mile to Main Street.

Here you can turn left and return to the Equinox, or turn right and then make a left onto River Road, which will take you out to the farms along the Batten Kill.

(From the Equinox around the loop back to the Equinox is about 1.2 miles. A walk down River Road to the river and back will add about another 4 miles.)

A walk up the drive to Hildene, located further south on the left (east) side of Main Street, is also pleasant.

Middletown Springs

MIDDLETOWN SPRINGS has gone from life as an early farming community through a heady period as a fashionable spa in the late 19th century back to a quiet rural village. It nestles among the hills of the Taconic Range, bypassed by major roads. A modern gas station awaiting scant traffic at the green stands in marked contrast to a large red brick 1814 house, a white-spired church from 1796, and an elaborately trimmed late Victorian house. Down the road children still attend the big, white 1904 schoolhouse, a four-sided clock atop its belfry.

The village originally served residents who farmed the hills along the winding valley of the Poultney River, which runs through town. In 1840 sheep outnumbered people six to one. Manufacturing became important beginning in 1857, when a local millwright built a factory on the river. For sixty years the factory produced his invention, a treadmill that used literal horsepower to mechanize farm jobs like threshing and churning. The same entrepreneur later discovered mineral springs next to the river, and in 1871 he built the five-story Montvert Hotel, where visitors could allegedly cure a pharmacologist's encyclopedia of ailments, including hay fever.

The Montvert Hotel is no more; it succumbed to fickle fashion in 1906 as mineral springs gave way to more recreational resorts. The springs still flow, however, and have a pleasant, refreshing taste. They are in a small wooded park south of the green on Burdock Avenue across the river from the site of the hotel, sheltered by a decorative reconstructed springhouse.

The country around the village is that of a river valley cutting through modest mountains, believed to be the long-ago tops of the Green Mountains, which intense crustal folding broke off and slid 10 or 15 miles to the southwest. The river curves in a rocky stream with fields alongside and green forested hills above. Cows still graze on small farms just outside the village as it merges seamlessly into countryside.

The Montvert Hotel is no more; it succumbed to fickle fashion in 1906
as mineral springs gave way to more recreational resorts.
The springs still flow, however, and have a pleasant, refreshing taste.

RT 140

Village green

dirt road

RT 133

BEGIN YOUR WALK at the green and head south along Vermont Route 133 (passing Burdock Avenue, the park, and springs on your left).

After crossing the river, continue to the edge of the village and make a right onto an unpaved road heading west.

Walk about a mile until the next intersection at the bridge, cross the bridge, and make a right heading east on the paved Vermont Route 140.

This will take you back into the village to the green. (From the green, around the loop, and back to the green: about 2.5 miles.)

North Bennington

NORTH BENNINGTON PROSPERED as an industrial center during the 19th and early 20th centuries, and a row of red brick and stone factories still line Paran Creek below, where water spills over a dam near the village center. Roads run downhill into the hub of the village, meeting at a little grassy triangle not far from the dam. There, classical white columns of the public library face the even bigger columns of the village store.

This village was first known in the 1700s as Haviland's Mills, after its founder, and then by the rather western-sounding name of Sage City, after Captain Moses Sage, an early industrialist. (The Sage City Symphony, an ambitious local all-volunteer orchestra, now carries on the name.) Cotton and marble-sawing mills dominated its initial fifty years, and in 1828, when it received its own post office, it became North Bennington.

Near the triangular green are the red brick library with a marble foundation, several large houses from the 19th century, and the unusually grand portico of Power's Market. Its four tall columns of considerable girth are not wood but stacked circles of painted bricks. At the north end of the village, the railroad station features a central tower with a large clock that tells the right time even though the trains don't run. It has been rehabilitated for offices in a stylish coat of rich red and green paint that highlights its florid Victorian style. But the Park-McCullough House (1865), a thirty-five-room mansion on broad lawns a block uphill from the village center, is the real Victorian gem of this village. The house is embellished with all the curvy wooden decorative additions available to the Victorian builder, and a veranda sweeps around it. A playhouse on the lawn echoes its architectural details, including the cupola. The building is now open to the public (May to mid-October, with tours and events), and plans are afoot to restore and care for its somewhat neglected archive and artifact collections.

Even though forested hills surround North Bennington, a few farms cultivate fields amid patches of woods in the Walloomsac River Valley. Three covered bridges span the river at points south of the village. The elaborate barn of the Park-McCullough House, with its cupolas and weather vanes, is a reminder that this industrialist's estate was also a farm, as was what became Bennington College nearby. This marriage of agriculture with industrial wealth is the legacy that North Bennington so well illustrates today.

Near the triangular green are the red brick library with a marble foundation,
several large houses from the 19th century,
and the unusually grand portico of Power's Market.

BEGIN YOUR WALK near the triangular green in the center of the village (on Vermont Route 67A).

Head uphill on West Street to the Park-McCullough mansion and turn left (south) on Park Street.

Follow this over a mile to within sight of the Henry Covered Bridge, but before the bridge turn right onto the un-paved Harrington Road and head northwest.

Again go over a mile and make a right at the next intersection onto un-paved Knapp Road.

This will lead straight back to Park-McCullough and the village center. (From the center through the loop and back to the center: 4.1 miles.)

Pawlet

*D*RIVING INTO PAWLET is a bit like looking through a kaleidoscope: the pieces don't quite line up. The tilted territory Pawlet inhabits makes for a two-tiered village. At its center the village splits. A couple of frame buildings with white-railed double porches mark the upper street, while a lower street veers off with a general store and a town hall further down. Flower Creek flows downhill behind the little village on its way to the Mettawee River just south of town.

Although it seems sleepy now, Pawlet in 1830 was one of the biggest manufacturing centers in Vermont, larger than Rutland. Power was harnessed by many waterwheels along Flower Creek, and shuttles flew on looms weaving cotton and woolen cloth. After the Civil War quarries in the western half of town made it a major slate-producing center. But farming in the fertile Mettawee Valley was the mainstay of residents throughout the century; in 1895 four factories produced cheese using milk from local farms.

At the center of Pawlet village is the brick general store, built around 1820 as a hotel. It perches above Flower Creek, and a window in the floor shows the creek cascading below. Early houses line the road south (Vermont Route 30), the most prominent being "Five Hearths," with its massive central chimney. On the lower road are the 1881 Town Hall, with its jaunty cupola, and the 1911 Pawlet Graded School. The most recent addition to the village is actually an old building, too—the South Wallingford Railroad Station, moved here to serve as a restaurant.

South and north of the village, in the broad valley of the Mettawee River, some of the best farmland in the state is dotted with red barns, silos, cornfields, and pasturing Holsteins. Thanks to the efforts of local farmers in partnership with the Mettawee Valley Conservation Project, much of this beautiful area is being preserved for agricultural use in perpetuity. Above the fields and pasture, the abrupt, wooded slopes of the Taconics rise, closing in the valley. This is one of those places in Vermont where farming seems to define the landscape completely, with humans and nature in harmonious balance.

Although it seems sleepy now, Pawlet in 1830 was one of the biggest manufacturing centers in Vermont, larger than Rutland. Shuttles flew on looms weaving cotton and woolen cloth.

BEGIN YOUR WALK at the general store in the village (at the intersection of Vermont routes 30 and 133).

Head down the lower road on the left side of the store, past the school and town hall, and out across the Mettawee River.

Continue up from the river, bear right, and continue on the Pawlet-Rupert Mountain Road as far as you like while it gains elevation and views across the valley.

Return by the same route. (It is easy and pleasant to travel out 2 miles or more on this road, so assume a round-trip of more than 4 miles.)

Plymouth Notch

WALK AROUND THIS TINY VILLAGE and it seems but a moment since Calvin Coolidge, a local boy, took the oath of office as president of the United States in his family's sitting room here at 2:47 a.m., August 3, 1923 by the light of a kerosene lamp. The death of President Warren Harding had caught the vice-president vacationing in this remote hilltop hamlet at the edge of his grandfather's fields.

Plymouth Notch owes its preservation to that circumstance. Otherwise, this farming village tucked into the high, hilly area east of the Green Mountains would almost certainly have disappeared as have two other 19th-century villages in the 5 square miles that make up the town of Plymouth. The cluster of buildings is now managed by the State of Vermont as a historic site, but the village retains the air of a real place. A ticket allows entrance to the buildings, open daily 9:30 a.m. to 5 p.m. mid-May to mid-October, and a public road runs through the village.

A short stroll here recalls many events in Calvin Coolidge's life. The family's modest, white, two-story house with black shutters and a front porch, furnished as it was on that dramatic night, sets the imagination to work. The bedroom in which Coolidge was born on the Fourth of July in 1872 is across the street in an unpainted ell attached to the general store his father then managed. In 1924 Calvin made the store's upper room his summer White House. Next door is the Union Christian Church, where he worshipped. It was erected in 1840 and its interior remodeled with local pine in 1890 in Carpenter Gothic style. The yellow clapboard Wilder House (now a coffee shop) was the childhood home of Coolidge's mother; its barn is now a museum of 19th-century farming.

The village itself is a fine example of a hilltop farming community that supported a few families on unpromising land cleared of native New England hardwood. Beyond the cheese factory (still operated by the president's son), the road quickly becomes woodsy and begins to climb, offering occasional glimpses over the hills. South of the village there is the quiet cemetery where Calvin Coolidge is buried in his family's plot. The seal of the presidency on the stone marker is the only thing that distinguishes his grave from any other.

The village is a fine example of a hilltop farming community that supported a few families on unpromising land cleared of native New England hardwood.

BEGIN YOUR WALK at the Visitor's Center in Plymouth Notch. From here you can take two short walks, one through and around the village and another through the meadow across 100A. Brochures for both walks are available at the visitors center, and the trails are mowed.

Alternate walks are out the road that heads west, past the cheese factory and back or down the road heading south across 100A, past the cemetery, and back.

Rupert and West Rupert

THESE SMALL AGRICULTURAL villages among the hills barely interrupt the countryside. Rupert has a single street of houses and two churches. West Rupert, slightly more bustling, revolves around a general store and post office, which draw people together for the daily ritual of mail and errands.

The Town of Rupert was chartered in 1761 and probably named for an English prince. Despite battles to the north and south during the American Revolution, residents did not flee this out-of-the-way spot. After Shays's Rebellion in Massachusetts in 1778, Daniel Shays even hid in the woods here for a while. Farming sustained residents throughout the 19th century, although the area became more accessible after construction of the railroad through the western portion of town in 1852.

In Rupert village most of the houses have barns. The simple white Congregational church, built between 1786 and 1794 and remodeled in 1859, sits across from a cornfield. The town meetinghouse next to it was built with the same plain lines in 1871. Town meetings took place upstairs, and school was held on the ground floor. It is still in use, now with a library upstairs. The other church on the street is the gray Methodist church (1884), with its prominent side clock tower.

The hub of West Rupert is the general store, with town offices and the post office in a wing. This white frame building with red trim and a slate mansard roof is a fine example of a mid-19th-century store. Two wooden benches with aging, faded metal advertisements bolted to them flank the door. A red brick school from 1825 with a slate roof is around the corner.

Mill Brook flows between the two villages, surrounded by the hills of the Taconic Range. These mountains, some of which rise rather abruptly, have densely wooded peaks that reach over 2,000 feet. The divide between the St. Lawrence and the Hudson River watersheds crosses the town, some rivers and brooks flowing south and some flowing north. Most all of the flat valley land is used fully for farming, and cows graze at the edges of the villages. This working rural landscape lends Rupert an open feeling in what is really a setting defined by mountains.

The hub of *West Rupert* is the general store, with town offices and the post office in a wing. This white frame building with red trim and a slate mansard roof is a fine example of a mid-19th-century store.

BEGIN YOUR WALK in Rupert and find the old railroad bed (sans tracks) on the northwest side of Vermont Route 153. Follow the rail bed, as the locals do, 2.25 miles from one village to the other. A round-trip walk from Rupert to West Rupert is 4.5 miles.

Townshend

*W*HEN SCHOOL LETS OUT, the two-acre Townshend green is alive with children and teenagers running, playing ball, and talking to friends, all in the shadow of a tall, white, 200-year-old church. With the elementary and high schools, town hall, shops, and houses surrounding it, this green is the heart of its village.

Prior to the American Revolution, Vermont was territory claimed by both New York and New Hampshire, and Townshend gained its name from a New York charter. Its earliest residents came from Brattleboro and established a rural farming community and town center much like many others in the interior of Windham County. Among the village's most important historical events were a series of devastating fires between 1886 and 1918 that changed its appearance repeatedly. The fires successively destroyed the buildings on all sides of the green except the Congregational church.

The most important building on the green remains the church, and its steeple is the first thing seen from any road. Originally built in 1790 for use by both town and church, dissenters in 1800 demanded that the town withdraw from the building. Nonetheless in 1803 the church leased the green to the town for public use as long as it would support the church on it. And so a bargain was struck that has given two centuries of Townshend residents a splendid building, virtually unchanged inside and out, as well as the green itself.

Other buildings around the green range from those with the elaborate wood trim of the late 19th century to the spare, modern lines of the new high school. All contribute to the unity of the green with a similar scale and setback. Most buildings, whether store or residence, maintain the white-with-trim color scheme that also adds to the coherence of the scene.

Steep, forested hills come right to the edge of the village, which is located in the West River Valley. To stop repeated floods, a 1,700-foot dam was built a few miles west of the village, which created a recreation area for the town. This hilly, rocky area has not remained hospitable to agriculture, but it is attractive to people who have bought old farmhouses for country living, maybe as a second home or a place to retire.

The Townshend green is the heart of the village.
The most important building on the green remains the church,
and its steeple is the first thing seen from any road.

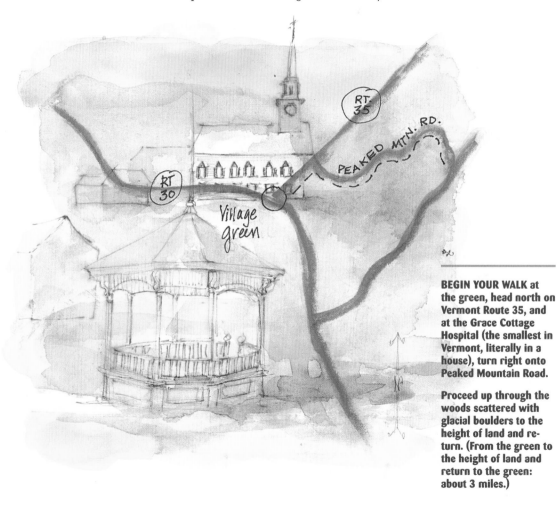

BEGIN YOUR WALK at the green, head north on Vermont Route 35, and at the Grace Cottage Hospital (the smallest in Vermont, literally in a house), turn right onto Peaked Mountain Road.

Proceed up through the woods scattered with glacial boulders to the height of land and return. (From the green to the height of land and return to the green: about 3 miles.)

Wallingford

*A*LTHOUGH FOUNDED BY FARMERS, Wallingford does not look like a farming village. That's because a pitchfork factory brought a century of wealth to the community, and the many substantial houses and solid commercial and public buildings on Main Street are the result. Although today a number of the fanciful Victorian-era houses are bed-and-breakfasts, the little stone factory is a gift shop, and the old inn is housing for the elderly, the outlines of the village's history remain intact in its fine collection of 19th-century architecture.

The confluence of Roaring Brook with Otter Creek and its broad fertile valley brought farmers to this hilly, forested frontier town beginning in 1780. They thrived by raising wheat and then Merino sheep in the valley, where large brick and clapboard houses with elaborate barns attest to their success. The water-power of Roaring Brook sustained a number of saw-mills and shops in the village, but after Wallingford became a stop on the Rutland and Bennington Railroad in 1852, industry greatly expanded. Pitch-forks and other wooden farming implements were manufactured and shipped to national markets. After 1910, as the market for farm implements declined, one manufacturer switched to golf clubs and snow-shoes before closing altogether during the Great Depression.

The village grew along the north-south stage road (Main Street), with late-19th-century houses filling in the spaces between the early farmhouses. The little brick 1818 schoolhouse is renamed for the local boy who founded Rotary International. An elaborate Victorian mansion is a showcase for decorative wood trim and has a matching gazebo. And the early commercial buildings are dressed up with roof brackets from the late 1800s. At the main intersection, a statue of a boy is the center of a fountain: he holds up his boot, which perpetually leaks a stream of water. Further south, near Church Street, the original rough-stone pitchfork factory has adapted easily over the years to a tea room and gift shop, its small size and fireplace giving it an almost domestic feel.

Wallingford lies along Otter Creek in what geologists call the Valley of Vermont, between the Taconic and Green Mountain ranges. The river runs north and the railroad north-south through the valley. With its historic farms and dramatic setting, the area south of the village has been listed in the National Register of Historic Places as Vermont's first rural historic district. The old stage road, now U.S. Route 7, retains a modest scale here as it dodges between farmhouses and barns. It is worth seeing before the road is "improved."

Wallingford does not look like a farming village. The outlines of the village's history remain intact in its fine collection of 19th-century architecture.

BEGIN YOUR WALK at the main intersection near "The Boy with the Leaking Boot" fountain.

From here head west on Depot Street and make the jog to cross the Otter Creek over the 1949 steel truss bridge on Vermont Route 140.

Then make your first left onto Waldo Lane, which follows the banks of the creek into the rural historic district.

When you reach the intersection with U.S. Route 7, turn around and return by the same route. (From the fountain to the intersection of Waldo Lane and U.S. 7 and return: about 2.2 miles.)

An alternate walk of about 5.5 miles round-trip is east on Church Street and then Vermont Route 140 (east) to the White Rocks Picnic Area (in the Green Mountain National Forest) and return.

Weston

*W*ESTON is a mountain village centered on what was a frog pond before the Civil War. Now it is a grassy green neatly bound by an ornamental iron fence—not to keep anyone out but to frame the picture. The bandstand and the imposing summer theater facing the green show the local taste for entertainment. Summer and fall, Weston is a magnet for visitors to the theater and the nearby Vermont Country Store, which trades in useful old-fashioned products and nostalgia.

Weston was settled in 1776, the last village at the northern end of the West River Valley, and it prospered into the next century, supplying goods and services to the town's 1,100 residents, most on outlying farms. There were sawmills and gristmills, carding mills and tanneries, blacksmith shops and a hotel. Then, in the manner of many hill towns, it declined in the latter half of the 19th century as mass-produced goods replaced those made locally. The village's revival began in the 1920s and 1930s, when people interested in restoring some of the old buildings moved to town and others established the Weston Playhouse.

On one side of the green, the simple dignity of the clapboard Farrar-Mansur House, a 1797 tavern that is now a museum of local history, attracts attention. Next door is the broad white expanse of the Weston Playhouse (1962), whose six-columned portico recalls that of the Congregational church, its original home. South of the green is an 1805 church, remod-

eled in the 1870s, when its unusual double-roofed bell tower was probably added. On the street west of the green stand two notable restorations: the Wilder Homestead (1827), a large red brick house with graceful arched window treatments, and the white Church on the Hill (1838), built for Baptists but restored 100 years later for members of all faiths.

The valley the village inhabits is a narrow one, banked by green hillsides. As in other places attractive to visitors fleeing modern sprawl, inhabitants manage to keep commercial activity within the village, leaving both it and the countryside much as they were. Forest has reclaimed most of the hill farms, and now the area is appealing to second-home owners or those who want to live a rural life. Any road that leads up from the West River rapidly lapses into thick forest, a reminder, if any were needed, that Weston is a Green Mountain town.

The village's revival began in the 1920s and 1930s,
when people interested in restoring some of the old buildings moved to town
and others established the Weston Playhouse.

BEGIN YOUR WALK at the green, go west past the Church on the Hill, and keep heading uphill to the right onto the Trout Club Road and then Lawrence Hill Road.

Go about a quarter mile and turn left onto Moses Pond Road, which takes you into the Green Mountain National Forest.

The pond is over 4 miles from the village green, so walk as far as you like and return by the same route.

Windham and South Windham

WINDHAM AND SOUTH WINDHAM lie almost 4 miles apart on a high road with forest on all sides in one of the highest towns in Vermont. Except for a church in each village, there are only a few houses, some old and some fairly recent, to indicate these are villages. Agricultural buildings almost outnumber the homes, a reflection of the villages' modest history as centers for a hill-farm community.

The simple, white frame Windham Congregational Church stands by the side of the road in a grove of trees. It is freshly painted white, with a spire, green shutters, and double doors. It was erected in 1802 in a single day by twenty men each from Windham, Peru, Weston, Londonderry, and Andover. In 1894 citizens made over the ground floor into the town hall and library. Behind the church is a plain, wood-frame house once the home of a 19th-century cabinetmaker and later the Congregational parsonage.

In South Windham the church is an unusual blend of brick and clapboard. It has red brick side and rear walls and a white clapboard front. Its series of recessed arches around the side windows was a common treatment in Vermont buildings between about 1814 and 1830. The three-tiered steeple is topped by a weather vane. As in Windham, next door is the old parsonage, another simple, white, wood-frame structure. The largest home in the village, the two-story Harrington House was built by that family about 1860 as their residence, cabinet shop and coffin factory.

A walk along the gentle decline from Windham to South Windham leads past Burbees Pond, from which Turkey Mountain Brook runs down to the West River and continues through a wooded landscape. The feeling here is of being on top of Vermont, walking the crest of a wooded ridge. The surrounding mountains are just a bit higher. It is a different perspective looking out rather than up at them. Once there were hill farms all along this route; the forest has largely reclaimed all. Major ski areas and their active, neighboring towns are not far away over the Green Mountains to the west, but Windham is not of that world.